TASC PUBLICATIO

GW01035602

POWER TO TH
Assessing Democracy in Ireland
Written and edited by
Ian Hughes, Paula Clancy, Clodagh Harris, and David Beetham 2007

POWER TO THE PEOPLE?
Assessing Democracy in Northern Ireland
by Rick Wilford, Robin Wilson and Kathleen Claussen 2007

TAMING THE TIGER
Social Exclusion in a Globalised Ireland
by David Jacobson, Peadar Kirby, and Deiric Ó Broin November 2006

GRIDLOCK
Dublin's transport crisis and the future of the city
by James Wickham June 2006

OUT OF REACH
Inequalities in the Irish Housing System
by PJ Drudy and Michael Punch December 2005

ENGAGING CITIZENS
The Report of the Democracy Commission
Edited by Clodagh Harris October 2005

POST WASHINGTON
Why America can't rule the World
by Tony Kinsella and Fintan O'Toole June 2005

FOR RICHER, FOR POORER
An investigation of the Irish Pension System
Edited by Jim Stewart May 2005

AN OUTBURST OF FRANKNESS
Community arts in Ireland – a reader
Edited by Sandy Fitzgerald November 2004

SELLING OUT?
Privatisation in Ireland
by Paul Sweeney October 2004

AFTER THE BALL
by Fintan O'Toole October 2003

TASC RESEARCH PAMPHLETS TO DATE

Public Perspectives on Democracy in Ireland
Topline Results
by Paula Clancy, Ian Hughes and Teresa Brannick June 2005

Outsourcing Government
public bodies and accountability
by Paula Clancy and Grainne Murphy May 2006

The Trouble with Northern Ireland
the belfast agreement and democratic governance
by Rick Wilford and Robin Wilson April 2006

tasc

A Think Tank for Action on Social Change
26 Sth Frederick St, Dublin 2.
Ph: 00353 1 6169050
Email:contact@tascnet.ie
www.tascnet.ie

democratic audit ireland

The Democratic Audit Ireland Project is a project of TASC – A Think Tank for Action on Social Change, initiated in 2004. It is the first comprehensive audit of democracy in Ireland. The objective of the audit is to analyse the strengths and weaknesses of Ireland's democracy, to chart progress, and to identify what most needs improving. As part of the project, TASC also commissioned a similar audit in Northern Ireland.

The full reports of the audits were published in May 2007:
Power to the People? Assessing Democracy in Ireland
Power to the People? Assessing Democracy in Northern Ireland.

In addition, a number of more detailed investigations of different aspects of democracy in each of the jurisdictions have been published over the last two years: a public opinion survey on attitudes and behaviour in relation to politics and democracy; a report on accountability and public bodies; and an in-depth analysis of the Good Friday Agreement of 1998. This pamphlet is the fourth such specialist investigation.

The methodology used in the audits is based on the International IDEA Assessment Framework. For further information on the Democratic Audit Ireland Project log on to www.tascnet.ie

Acknowledgements

The authors are indebted to the contributions of Mark Callanan, Peadar Kirby, Mary Murphy, Liam Kelly, Chris O'Malley and Odran Reid. We are also grateful to Paula Clancy for her patience and support, and to lan Hughes and Clodagh Harris for their constructive advice.

Governing
Below the Centre:
local governance in Ireland

June 2007
Deiric Ó Broin
Eugene Waters

Copyright: © TASC, 2007

Governing Below the Centre
First published 2007
by tasc at New Island
an imprint of New Island Press
2 Brookside
Dundrum
Dublin 14

www.newisland.ie

ISBN 978-1-905494-87-3.

British Library Cataloguing in Publication Data.
A CIP catalogue record for this book is available
from the British Library.

Typeset by Ashfield Press
Cover design by Public Communications Centre

Printed in Ireland by
Betaprint Limited, Dublin

Contents

AUTHORS

DEIRIC Ó BROIN is the Director of NorDubCo, a regional 'think and do' tank based in Dublin City University. For some years previously he was employed as an economic policy analyst in the private sector. He has written a number of articles on local governance and local development in Ireland, and was an editor of *Taming the Tiger – Social Exclusion in a Globalised Ireland*.

EUGENE WATERS is a principal officer at the Member Services Unit of the London Borough of Newham. He holds a BA (Hons) in Human Development from St. Patrick's College, Drumcondra and an MRes in European Public Policy from Birkbeck, University of London.

ABBREVIATIONS

ADM	Area Development Management
AIT	Area Implementation Team
BAP	Blanchardstown Area Partnership
CDB	County/City Development Board
CDP	Community Development Programme
CDSP	Community Development Support Programme
CEB	County/City Enterprise Board
CLÁR	Ceantair Laga Árd-Riachtanais/Programme for Revitalising Rural Areas
CPA	Combat Poverty Agency
CRAGA	Department of Community, Rural and Gaeltacht Affairs
DCC	Dublin City Council
DEHLG	Department of the Environment, Heritage and Local Government
DSFA	Department of Social and Family Affairs
EI	Enterprise Ireland
ERHA	Eastern Regional Health Authority
EU	European Union
FÁS	Foras Áiseanna Saothair/National Manpower Agency
FDI	Foreign Direct Investment
GDA	Greater Dublin Area
HSE	Health Service Executive
IAP	Integrated Area Plan
IBEC	Irish Business and Employers Confederation
ICT	Information and Communications Technology
ICTU	Irish Congress of Trade Unions
IDA	Industrial Development Authority Ireland
IFA	Irish Farmers Association
LAC	Local Area Committee
LDSIP	Local Development Social Inclusion Programme

LDTF	Local Drugs Task Force
LES	Local Employment Service
NDP	National Development Programme
NGO	Non-Governmental Organisation
NESC	National Economic and Social Council
NESDO	National Economic and Social Development Office
NESF	National Economic and Social Forum
NRA	National Roads Authority
OPLURD	Operational Programme for Local, Urban and Rural Development
PWS	Probation and Welfare Service
RAPID	Revitalising Areas through Planning, Investment and Development
RPANI	Review of Public Administration Northern Ireland
SPC	Strategic Policy Committee
VEC	Vocational Education Committee

LIST OF TABLES

LIST OF FIGURES

Foreword

BY PEADAR KIRBY

The importance of local government has been consistently undervalued by scholars of Irish politics. While not entirely neglected in surveys of the Irish political system, it has never emerged as a subject deemed worthy of sustained study by professional political scientists, and political journalists treat it largely as a subject of minor importance which is of interest to a local audience but not significant in the context of the major issues of national politics. Yet, few in Ireland seem to realise that, when compared to experiences in regions throughout the world, this neglect of the structures and practice of local democracy is very unusual. The most successful states – successful in giving voice to their citizens and responding effectively to their needs, but also in being examples of sustained and equitable socio-economic development – are characterised by robust forms of local democracy. As a scholar of Latin American politics, I have witnessed the widespread and innovative reforms of local government throughout the region over the past two decades, reforms that have reinforced the quality of democracy in those countries and have played no small role in the emergence of the wave of 'new left' governments that is now capturing attention worldwide. Many of the leaders of these governments and the ruling parties of the left first emerged to prominence in local politics, where they gained the support and experience that laid the basis for their success at national, and now international, level.

In Ireland, by contrast, the tendency has been not so much to reform local government in any thorough and innovative way but, rather, to establish new institutions to try to plug the gaps in what is a patently dysfunctional system, so as to overcome the obstacles to effective governance that it presents. As Dublin city manager, John Tierney, wrote in a previous TASC publication, local government in Ireland 'is fragmented and in many instances distant and unaccountable. We have the narrowest range of functions delivered under the local government umbrella in Europe so there is no local accountability, for example in relation to the delivery of education and public transport'. He added that new bodies such as County and City Development Boards, Community Fora and Strategic Policy Committees, while demonstrating potential, need to be accompanied by a devolution of power from central government (Tierney, 2006: 65, 66). Yet, instead of this happening, we have seen a modest proposal for directly-elected mayors, something that has helped greatly to reinvigorate local, and indeed, national politics throughout Latin America, being defeated by opposition within Fianna Fáil. Furthermore, what passes for 'decentralisation' in Irish politics is simply the scattering of parts of a highly centralised administration to the provinces in a way that has little logic except the electoral needs of Fianna Fáil and the Progressive Democrats and that does absolutely nothing to decentralise power.

Indeed, if the democratic imperatives for reforming the structures of local government have not been sufficient to persuade the power elites of Irish society to give greater priority to the task, then the demands of globalisation should be concentrating the minds of those who govern us. For there is a widespread recognition that, as Anthony Giddens has put it, 'local transformation is as much a part of globalisation as the lateral extension of social connections across time and space' (Giddens, 2000: 92). This process of global forces transforming local spaces is all too much a reality in contemporary Ireland as decisions made in boardrooms in the US, Germany or Japan result in an immediate, and sometimes devastating, impact on personal livelihoods and local economies in many towns and townlands across Ireland. The recognition of this new importance that the local has taken on in a globalised world has resulted in a lively literature on the importance of localisation namely, as Hines puts it, 'that governments provide the policy framework which allows people and businesses to rediversify their own local economies' (Hines, 2000: 29). In other words, power needs to be devolved down to local communities to help them respond effectively to the vulnerabilities and volatility of today's global flows, an argument that is well made in the pages that follow. For a society that depends so much for its prosperity on such global flows, it is foolhardy in the extreme for policymakers to neglect the difficult task of building effective organs of local governance. Yet that is precisely where we find ourselves as we face the daunting challenges of post-Celtic Tiger Ireland.

This, then, provides the context for this very welcome publication. Forming part of the Democratic Audit of Ireland being undertaken by TASC, this pamphlet fills a huge gap in providing an accessible and comprehensive introduction to the administrative maze that substitutes for local government in Ireland. It is very informative in describing the wide array of local bodies or national bodies with local responsibilities, how they relate or don't relate to one another, and the worrying deficit that results in terms of holding them accountable for outcomes at local level. The authors go further in arguing with effectiveness the case both for a real devolution of power to local level and for wider revenue-raising powers for local government. Furthermore, they very tellingly compare Irish local and regional government to that in other European countries in terms of the functions allocated to government at these levels, their share of public employment and the average population that constitutes the lowest tier of sub-national government. Under all headings, Ireland emerges as a highly centralised state.

This work deserves a very wide readership, both among students of Irish politics and development and also among the wider public who are interested in how forms of governance may help in the continuing and ever more intensified challenges of maintaining a successful economy and addressing the huge social deficits that so tarnish the face of today's Ireland. Furthermore, in drawing together such an array of valuable information about the functions and operations of the many agencies it identifies that have responsibility for some aspect of local development, this pamphlet is an invaluable work of reference that will ensure it a long life. The authors are to be commended on an admirable job of research and synthesis presented in a very accessible way. It is to be hoped that it not only informs the public about the alarmingly dysfunctional state of Irish local governance but also that it motivates a badly needed pressure for thorough reform.

PEADAR KIRBY *is Associate Professor at the School of Law and Government in Dublin City University.*

Introduction

The state of local democracy in Ireland has been a matter of concern for some period of time. Attempts at reform have been memorably described as "a false pregnancy that has lasted since 1971 at least" (Barrington, 1991: 163). There have been a number of attempts to reform local government but substantial concerns about the condition of local democracy in Ireland remain, particularly in light of the increasing centralisation of decision-making. In this paper we focus on those public agencies operating at local level and examine their relationship with regional, national and EU levels. The paper also examines the relationships at local level between local government and other local public agencies, in particular the impact of these relationships on local democracy.

The paper sets out the findings of research into the role and operation of the local governance process in Ireland and is a component of the Democratic Audit Ireland. A paper *Outsourcing Government – public bodies and accountability* examining the role of public agencies at national level has already been published.

This paper is broken into five parts. The first examines the context in which local governance occurs in Ireland and recent changes in the broader socio-economic and political environment. The second provides a brief overview of Irish local governance and local government, in particular the range of functions available to local public agencies and the levels at which these functions operate. This is followed by an examination of the extent and nature of citizen involvement in decision making. The penultimate section of the paper assesses the Irish experience of local governance. The paper concludes with a brief summary of its key conclusions and their implications for local democracy in Ireland.

The primary aim of the paper is to explore how governance processes operate at the local level and to assess the implications of this analysis for the future of local democracy in Ireland. Within the context of exploring how governance structures work at local level in Ireland, a number of specific research objectives were devised. These include:

(a)   Building a profile of local governance throughout the country, by mapping all the elected and non-elected organisations involved in public administration at the local level, including the relationships between different levels of administration, local, regional, national and European. A table detailing the results of this mapping exercise is contained in Appendix I.

(b)   Identifying the various forms of accountability for each type of organisation and mapping the formal ways in which citizens can have an influence on decision making. A description of these is contained in Appendix II.

In seeking to meet these objectives, a series of research questions under both of the broader research objectives are considered:

(a)   What are the primary responsibilities of local agencies?

(b)   When were these agencies established and what was the formal rationale for establishing them?

(c)   How much money does each agency spend locally, how do they determine how to spend it and what are the sources of finance?

(d)   What is the relationship between the local, regional, national and European levels of governance?

(e)   How are local policy priorities arrived at?

(f)   How much of a say do local residents have in relation to these decisions?

These questions formed the basis of the research and have guided the structure of the paper.

The nature of information gathered has presented some problems of how best to present the paper's findings (see Appendix IV for an overview of the methodology employed). One such concerns the complexity of the governance structure. Ireland's governance structure involves a large number of agencies (491) operating in overlapping areas. There are three very broad levels of operation:

(a) Sub-city/county, for example town councils, some area partnerships, port authorities and RAPID and CLÁR programmes;
(b) City/county, for example city and county councils, city/county development boards, city/county enterprise boards and VECs;
(c) Quasi-regional, for example regional assemblies, regional authorities, Health Service Executive regional structures and Department of Education and Science regional structures (all of whose regional areas are different).

A second issue is that of the difficulty of locating the Irish case in an international context. Ireland's system of local governance does not easily facilitate international comparisons, primarily because of the paucity of research data available. In those aspects of local governance where Ireland does not have a directly comparable structure or level of activity, we have attempted to provide what we considered the most appropriate comparator.

Thus, while we have worked to ensure that where possible these issues are identified and explained, it is likely that there will be some disagreements about our presentation of the data. With this in mind we hope that this paper will be seen as the first step in a dialogue and we hope we will be able to work with stakeholders to develop a richer picture of local governance in Ireland.

Executive Summary

1. CHANGES IN THE BROADER SOCIO-ECONOMIC AND POLITICAL ENVIRONMENTS

Local public agencies have seen significant transformations in their external socio-economic and political environments. These include urbanisation, globalisation and Europeanisation. In addition, local public agencies have been confronted with new challenges by their local communities. These include demands for new and more efficient services and demands for greater citizen and community participation in decision-making processes.

These changes suggest two linked challenges for local public agencies. First, the rise of more demanding and more critical citizens forces local public agencies to improve their capacity for more effective and efficient governance. Arguably this should make them more receptive to (a) the adoption of innovative management techniques and recruitment and promotion options and (b) the involvement of new stakeholders, including community-based organisations, in an effort to improve their problem-solving ability. This in turn creates new challenges for local public agencies. Second, new participatory demands, the decline in voter turnout and the partial decline of traditional political party linkages (for example the growth of successful independent candidates) require local public agencies to think about new channels of communication with local communities and to consider new forms of local democracy.

2. LOCAL GOVERNANCE AND LOCAL GOVERNMENT IN IRELAND

The local governance process in Ireland is characterised by a large number of agencies (22 distinct types totalling 491 across the country), operating in overlapping areas. There are three very broad levels of operation: sub-city/county, for example town councils, some area partnerships, port authorities and RAPID and CLÁR programmes; city/county, for example city and county councils, city/county development boards, city/county enterprise boards and VECs; and quasi-regional, for example regional assemblies, regional authorities, Health Service Executive regional structures and Department of Education and Science regional structures (all of whose regional areas are different).

Despite the existence of a substantial sub-national governance infrastructure, the vast majority of public expenditure decisions continue to be made at national level (approximately 94 per cent). In addition a wide range of services delivered at local level are managed and planned by national organisations with little or no local or regional autonomy. As a result, local governments in Ireland have a drastically reduced set of functions in comparison to their European counterparts. However, despite this, local governments are responsible for the vast majority of locally-accountable public expenditure decisions at local level (approximately 90 per cent). Finally, there is a significant amount of overlapping boundaries between agencies and questions about the continuing relevance of a number of agencies.

3. LOCAL DEMOCRACY IN IRELAND

The paper finds that locally-elected public representatives in Ireland play a much reduced role in policy-formulation and decision-making processes than their European counterparts and the ability of citizens to influence either of these processes beyond casting their ballot is very narrow. This reflects the powerful role of the city/county manager in Irish local government, the narrow range of services delivered by local government and the unusually small number of councils elected in Ireland.

4. THE EXPERIENCE OF LOCAL GOVERNANCE AND LOCAL DEMOCRACY IN IRELAND

The last twenty years have seen the establishment of a number of new public and quasi-public agencies[1] at local level in Ireland. However, while there now appears to be more stakeholders and agencies in existence there is no perceptible increase in legitimate public scrutiny at local level. Furthermore, a key aspect of the local governance process is its interactivity. It is interactive because no single agency has the knowledge and resource capacity to tackle problems unilaterally. This feature has not been included as an institutional design principle and as a result attempts to provide an appropriate institutional architecture for local governance processes have been flawed.

In addition, a point generally accepted in the rest of the EU, that some power of local taxation is essential for local government to retain some degree of autonomy, remains unresolved in Ireland. For example, approximately 50 per cent of local government funding comes from central coffers. Rates, service charges and development levies account for the remainder. This substantially reduces the ability of local governments and the communities they serve to address local problems in a flexible and appropriate manner.

5. THE IMPLICATIONS FOR LOCAL DEMOCRACY IN IRELAND

This paper does not contend that local governments always act fairly and effectively or that central government is always autocratic and inefficient. The argument is simply that of pluralism: when there are several centres of relatively autonomous power, disagreements are likely to come into the open and open government is preferable to the coteries of centralism.

What if the current vogue for active citizenship included a role for powerful and critical citizens and this vision was given real clarity and focus – with a system of local governance designed to have the structure, functions, resources and politics that could deliver it. This paper argues that a more transparent, devolved and accountable system of local governance is required and that local government has the key role to play in that system.

Notes

1   The use of the terms 'public agency' and 'quasi-public agency' require clarification. We found it useful to use the term 'public agency' when referring to agencies established by legislation or statutory instrument and 'quasi-public agency' when referring to the organisations which are allocated and expend public monies but which are constituted as private limited liability companies. Some of relevant literature uses the term 'quasi-private' to refer to such agencies (Denters and Rose, 2005: 252) but in the Irish context we did not feel that this was useful.

Changes in the broader socio-economic and political environments

Ireland along with most contemporary democracies has seen major changes in the contexts in which local decision making takes place.[1] First, local public agencies have seen significant transformations in their external socio-economic and political environments. These include urbanisation, globalisation and Europeanisation. In addition, local public agencies have been confronted with new challenges by their local communities, for example, demands for new and more efficient services and demands for greater citizen and community participation in decision-making processes.

URBANISATION

At its simplest, urbanisation refers to increases in the percentages of the national population living in urban places. It is not a new phenomenon and in Ireland has long historical roots. Nonetheless, it is a process that has dramatically increased in pace over the course of the past fifteen years and shows every likelihood of continuing in to the future. It poses particular problems for the Greater Dublin Area (Dublin City, Fingal, Dún Laoghaire-Rathdown, South County Dublin, Meath, Kildare and Wicklow) and also presents major problems for Cork, Galway, Limerick, Kilkenny and Waterford. Theorists such as Manuel Castells suggest that urbanisation is one of the key spatial processes of the early twenty first century. He contends that the end result will be the development of a set of urbanised villages that are part of the "urban constellations scattered throughout huge territorial expanses" (2002: 549). While many thinkers debate the positive and negatives aspects of these processes, we believe it is obvious that, at least at some level, Ireland's east coast is experiencing aspects of the process that Castells describes (Byrne, 2003: 352-370).

GLOBALISATION

For those involved in the process of local governance, the ongoing development of an international and globalised economic and social order presents numerous challenges. Promises of free trade, open borders, industrial restructuring, labour mobility, technology transfer and the ICT revolution create both remarkable opportunities and substantial challenges. In light of these developments, many commentators contend that effective local governance will be increasingly important in the realm of economic development because globalisation (and Europeanisation as outlined below) tend to undermine the nation state's traditional macro-economic policies (Gaffikin and Morrissey, 1999: 20-21; Savitch, 2003: 27-29; Clarke, 2003: 34-36). We are not suggesting that the nation state is by any means defunct rather that changes in "trade, production and financial internationalisation add up to a qualitatively new era of capitalism" (Munck, 2003: 5) and these developments have resulted in a level of economic internationalisation that has achieved an unprecedented depth and extension. As a result, most nation states have changed and are in the process of changing how they engage with globalisation. We suggest that it is at the local level that much of this new form of engagement will occur.

As a result local public agencies are becoming, and will continue to become more prominent in the economic policy domain. For example, while local governments in the United States have traditionally played a very active part in the development and implementation of economic development policies, many of their Irish counterparts are only beginning to consolidate a role, beyond their traditional zoning function, in this important area. Some local governments have been proactive in this area, for example the establishment of the Donegal Employment Task Force,[2] but in general local governments are slow to articulate a role for themselves in this area in comparison to their European Union, Australian or New Zealand counterparts. These new circumstances also raise the issue of the local political agenda. What for example, are the priorities of local public agencies with regard to economic development, social inclusion and environmental concerns? In addition, there are concerns that the evolving Irish local governance system lacks the appropriate policy and legislative framework, as well as the human capital, to develop adequate responses to these pressures (Adshead, 2003: 118).

EUROPEANISATION

Within the European Union the process of integration is becoming increasingly important for local governance. Local public agencies may be directly affected by EU policies when these policies imply rules and regulations that impact on their activities or when the EU provides new sources of funding for local programmes. In addition there is also a variety of indirect effects. For example, in a number of ways, the EU has changed the balance of power between central and local government. Partly stimulated by EU subsidies, many local public agencies have also broadened their horizons and become more active in numerous international networks and partnerships (Callanan, 2003b: 404-428).

NEW DEMANDS

Recent years have also seen significant changes within local communities, changes that have influenced their relationships with local public agencies. There is a discernible change in citizens' attitudes towards local (and central) public agencies: evidence suggests that attitudes are being increasingly influenced by instrumental considerations concerning the efficacy of public agencies in meeting citizen demands. In addition, there has been marked increase in the personal skills and educational attainment of citizens and an associated rise in demands for participation. Ireland is the latest in a long list of countries to witness this trend. As Denters and Rose note "with increased education more people have acquired politically-relevant skills and a sense of political competence, characteristics which in many instances result in demands for more extensive opportunities for political participation going beyond that of voting" (2005: 5). Concurrently, there has been a marked decline in traditional electoral participation.[3] While there are competing explanations for the decline in mass citizen involvement, an enduring consequence is the increasing lack of legitimacy accorded to public decisions by many citizens and communities.

These changes suggest two linked challenges for local public agencies. First, the rise of more demanding and more critical citizens forces local public agencies to improve their capacity for more effective and efficient governance. Arguably, this should make the public agencies more receptive to (a) the adoption of innovative management techniques and recruitment and promotion options and (b) the involvement of new stakeholders, including community-based organisations and new communities, in an effort to improve their problem-solving ability. Second, new participatory demands, the decline in voter turnout and the partial decline of traditional political party linkages (for example, the growth of successful independent candidates) require local public agencies to think about new channels of communication with local communities and to consider new forms of local democracy.

Notes

1   The study team found it helpful to use Denters and Rose's typology (2005, 2-9) to discuss these changes.

2   The Donegal Employment Task Force was established on the 16th September 1998 in response to significant job losses in Donegal. Among the wide variety of activities undertaken to help the development agencies sell Donegal locations to prospective inward investors, was the creation of a £5M (€6,348,690) Economic Development Fund by Donegal County Council. This fund was created to underpin the work and recommendations from the Donegal Employment Initiative Task Force Report. The Economic Development Fund is both a countywide and a rolling fund, which is replenished by returns on the Council's investment in economic and job creating investments.

3   The 2004 local elections confounded this trend. The turnout increased to 59.9 per cent. In particular the turnout in the Dublin region increased from 36 per cent in the 1999 local elections to 53 per cent in 2004. It is argued that a significant proportion of the increase was down to the fact that a referendum on citizenship was held at the same time (Kavanagh, 2004: 64-84).

Local governance and local government in Ireland

reland's system of local government is very much influenced by history and the population distribution in the country. Ireland has a fairly low-density population, the distribution of which is skewed towards the eastern coast. The Irish system of local government was inherited from Britain in 1922 and has experienced very little change since. Moreover, local government in Ireland has helped shape Ireland's particular political culture. This culture had its roots in the late 19th century and the development of the national independence movement. It retains a rather conservative outlook towards institutional innovation. This has resulted in key stakeholders being loathe to give up the comfort, stability and predictability of the status quo. For example the main function of Ireland's two regional assemblies is to facilitate the drawing down of EU regional development funding. They do not represent a central government belief in the efficacy of devising a coherent regional tier of governance. Given this context it is not surprising that Ireland is generally recognised as being one of the most centralised Member States in the European Union.

LOCAL GOVERNANCE

In order to map the structure of local governance in Ireland, it is helpful to start by defining our terms. This paper seeks to examine and assess local governance rather than just local government, which is just one component, though without doubt the most significant component, of the larger picture. It is important to note that many services delivered at local level and many of the decisions which affect local communities are not under the control of the relevant town, borough, city or county council, but other public bodies such as the National Roads Authority, Department of Education and Science or the Health Services Executive. Moreover, many important local decisions require the active co-operation of a number of public agencies. In addition, some decision-making powers have been repatriated to central government departments or insulated from the influence of elected councillors. In this context we found it helpful to view local governance as a process involving multi-agency working and partnerships that cut across organisational boundaries. As such, local governance in Ireland involves local government plus the looser processes of influencing and negotiating with a range of public and private stakeholders to achieve desired outcomes. A local governance perspective illustrates collaboration between agencies to achieve mutual goals. In essence, there is an acceptance that no one agency can effectively exercise hierarchical power over another. As a result, the governance process is interactive because no single agency, public or private, has the knowledge and resource capacity to tackle the key problems unilaterally (Kooiman, 1993: 4-6; Kooiman, 2003: 5).

LOCAL GOVERNMENT

In examining the term local government, it is important to note how the usage in Ireland is rather different to that employed by many of our fellow European Union Member States. For example, the term local government implies that it is local and government. Neither term is simple in its content. First, considerable argument has taken place about the nature of "local". For some it implies an area consecrated by long history and tradition: the counties and urban settlements that structure our formal spatial awareness. For, others, the appropriate locality for local government purposes is the socio-economic area, governed by journeys to work and the scale needed to provide certain public services. From both perspectives "local" is understood as wider in scope in Ireland than in many other systems of local government (see Table 1 for more detail). Second, there is the problem of defining "government". Local governments are not sovereign bodies and, while there are now certain constitutional protections in place, for example, the stricture that local governments must be established and elections must be held every five years, their powers are determined by the Oireachtas. The Oireachtas retains a constitutional sovereignty enabling it to change or to revoke previously-enacted legislation affecting local government. Local governments depend upon statute and were, up until 1991, subject to a strict interpretation of the legal rule of *ultra vires*. Since the passing of the Local Government Act 1991 local governments have had a 'general competence'. This was reiterated in section 66 of the Local Government Act 2001. However, this power is in the main hypothetical, as most local governments don't have the financial resources to fund new initiatives.

Local governments are elected bodies and are expected to develop policies appropriate to their localities within the framework of national legislation. There is a common understanding of the meaning of local government in the Irish context. First, local governments have a clearly defined physical structure: they have geographical boundaries that are contiguous but do not overlap. No part of the state is either excluded from at least one tier of government or is included in the territory of two local governments of the same status.

Second, local governments are multi-purpose bodies responsible for a number of services, although these are quite narrow in comparison to other EU Member States (see Table 1 for more detail). Third, local governments are directly elected on a similar franchise to that used for Dáil elections. Fourth, local governments have an independent power, albeit carefully circumscribed, of raising taxation.

In this regard, it is appropriate to use the term local government as referring to the local formal institutions of the state (county, city, borough and town councils). It is also important to note that Ireland has a number of regional agencies or national agencies with a regional focus, but not what can be described as a regional tier of governance because the regional authorities and regional assemblies, despite the fact that they are statutory agencies, are in essence networks of local governments and lack any real functions of their own. By contrast, local governments do make decisions within specific administrative and legal frameworks and use public resources in a financially accountable way.

In this study the term "local government" will only be used to describe county, city, borough and town councils. As noted earlier the term "local public agencies" will be used to describe the variety of public agencies, including local government, operating at local level in Ireland. This includes City/County Development Boards, City/County Enterprise Boards, etc. The term "local quasi-public agencies" will be used to refer to area partnerships, LEADER+ groups, local drugs task forces etc.

Table 1: Functions Allocated to Local and Regional Government within the EU

Functional Classification	Germany	Austria	France	Sweden	UK	Netherlands	Belgium	Denmark	Ireland
Refuse Collection and Disposal	L	L	L	L	L	L	L	L	L
Slaughterhouses	L	L	L	L	L	L	L	L	L
Theatres/Concerts	L,R	L,R	L	L	L	L	L	X	X
Museums, Libraries etc	L,R	L	L,R	L,R	L	L	L,R	L,R	L
Parks/Public Spaces	L	L	L,R	L	L	L,R	L,R	L	L
Sports and Leisure	L,R	L	L	L	L	L,R	L,R	L	L
Roads	L,R	L,R	L,R	L	L	L,R	L,R	L,R	L
Urban Road Transport	L,R	L	L,R	L,R	L	L	X	L	X
Ports	L,R	X	X	L	X	L	L	X	X
Airports	R	X	X	L,R	L	L	X	X	X
District Heating	L	L	L	L	X	L	L	L	X
Water Supply	L	L	L	L	L(a)	L,R	L	L	L
Agriculture, Fishing, Hunting, Forestry	L,R	R	L,R	L	L	L	L,R	X	X
Electricity	L	X	X	L	X	L,R	L,R	L	X
Commerce	L,R	L,R	L	L	X	L,R	L	X	X
Tourism	L,R	L,R	L,R	L,R	L	L	L,R	X	X
Security/Police	L,R	L	L	X	L	L,R	L	X	X
Fire Protection	L	L	L,R	L	L	L	L	L	L
Justice	R	X	X	X	L	X	X	X	X
Pre-School Education	L	L,R	L	L	L	L	L	L	X
Primary and Secondary Education	L,R	L,R	L (b)	L	L	L	L,R	L,R	X
Vocational and Technical Training	L	R	L	L,R	L	L	L,R	X	X
Higher Education	R	X	X	X	L	X	L,R	X	X
Adult Education	L,R	L	L	L,R	L	L	L	L	X
Hospitals and Convalescent Care	L,R	L,R	L,R	R	X	L,R	L,R	R	X
Personal Health	L,R	L,R	L	R	X	L	L	L,R	X
Family Welfare Services	L,R	L,R	L,R	L	L	L	L,R	L	X
Welfare Homes	L	L,R	L	L	L	L	L	L	X
Housing	L,R	L,R	L	L	L	L,R	L	X	L
Town Planning	L	L	L	L	L	L,R	L	L	L

Source: Adapted from Coughlan and de Buitleir, 1996: 6-7

L = Local Governments
R = Regional Governments (including State Governments; Departments in France; Provinces in Italy)
(a) Scotland Only
(b) Mainly Primary

Table 2: Share of Public Employment by Level of
Government (percentages in 1994)

Country	Level of Government	%	Rank in order of Local Size
Finland	Central	25.0	1
	Local	75.0	
Norway	Central	26.0	2
	Local	74.0	
Denmark	Central	27.1	3
	Local	70.8	
United Kingdom	Central	47.7	4
	Local	52.3	
Sweden*	Central	17.3	5
	Local (a)	52.9	
Germany	Federal	11.9	6
	Lander	51.0	
	Local	37.1	
Netherlands	Central and Other	72.4	7
	Local and Provinces	27.6	
Belgium	Central	33.2	8
	Regions and Communities	39.9	
	Local and Provincial	26.8	
France*	Central (b)	74.4	9
	Sub-National	18.4	
Greece	Central (c)	85.3	10
	Local	14.7	
Italy	Central	63.0	11=
	Regional	23.0	
	Local	14.0	
Portugal	Central	86.0	11=
	Local	14.0	
Spain*	Central	47.1	11=
	Regional	31.4	
	Local	24.0	
Ireland	**Central**	**87.3**	
	Local	**12.7**	**14**

Source: Adapted from John, 2001: 38

(a)   Includes the autonomous communes.
(b)   Includes health.
(c)   Excludes public establishments and public enterprises.
* Figures don't total 100% as employment data is not comparable in these cases.

Table 3: Average Population of Lowest Tier of Sub-National Government

Country	Average Population of Lowest Tier	Number of Councils (including all Tiers)
France	1,491	36,880
Portugal	2,342	4,526
Switzerland	2,352	3,021
Netherlands	2,723	584
Italy	7,182	8,215
Belgium	11,000	601
Finland	11,206	455
Denmark	18,000	289
Sweden	33,000	333
Ireland	**36,100**	**114**
United Kingdom	137,000	472

Source: Adapted from John, 2001: 35

Figure 1: Number and Level of Operations of Sub-National Governance in Ireland

2	Regional Assemblies (Border, Midlands and Western Regional Assembly & South and East Regional Assembly)
8	Regional Authorities (Border, Dublin, Mid East, Midlands, Mid West, South East, South West and West)
34	County/City level organisations (29 counties and 5 cities): County/City Councils, Development Boards, Vocational Education Committees* and Enterprise Boards
75	Town Councils
38	Area Partnerships, 33 Community Partnerships and 22 LEADER+ Groups
14	Drugs Task Force Areas (Dublin, Cork and Bray)
25	RAPID areas and 25 CLÁR areas

* The County Dublin Vocational Educational Committee has responsibility for vocational education in County Fingal, County South Dublin and part of Dún Laoghaire-Rathdown.

Local Democracy in Ireland

In examining how local policy priorities are determined, this paper notes the following:

(a)   the continuing pivotal role played by local governments in the various local policy-formulation processes;
(b)   the powerful role of the manager within local governments;
(c)   the relatively limited role of councillors and the opportunities available for local citizens to engage in local decision-making processes; and
(d)   the distance between councils, elected councillors and local citizens.

THE MANAGERIAL SYSTEM

With regard to the involvement of local governments in local policy-formulation processes, it is helpful to understand the process of decision making in Irish local governments. As noted earlier, there has been little institutional innovation in Irish local government. The first and probably most significant exception was the introduction and ongoing consolidation of the managerial system. This system constitutes a major difference between Ireland and other EU member states and has been the subject of substantial debate since its introduction in 1929. Despite recent proposals to introduce directly-elected mayors, the system remains largely unchanged. Yet the managerial system has had substantial impact on the ability of local citizens, through their elected councillors, to drive a particular policy agenda. In essence it has resulted in a democratic deficit where many decisions and policies are initiated and implemented by a non-elected manager. Decision making in Irish local governments can be broadly divided into two categories:

(a)　reserved functions which refer to those made by the elected representatives of the council;
(b)　executive functions which refer to those carried out by the county/city manager.

The main conclusion is that what has tended to happen is that the power of initiative has been granted to the manager and the majority of decisions made by the local government tend to lie in his/her domain. This is not to demean or underestimate the work carried out by managers but it remains problematic that managers are to a large extent insulated from the democratic deliberations of elected councillors. This has added to the public perception that local governments are an "invisible layer of government" (Keogan and Callanan, 2003: 503) with little relevance to people's daily lives. This perceived lack of relevance comes from a number of sources, including: the "cultural domination of national politics and government in Irish society" (Keogan and Callanan, 2003: 503); the fact that local governments are only tangentially involved in such vital services as health, education and policing; and the relative lack of power accorded to elected councillors. In essence, the managerial system has often given the impression that managers are there to protect the public from the shenanigans of their elected councillors, although it has also been suggested that many councillors are quite comfortable with managers taking the tough decisions, thus escaping the public fallout from such decisions.

We argue that the extent of managerial powers undermines the legitimate representative and scrutiny role of elected councillors. Scrutiny is one "key avenue for councillors to involve themselves in local government decision-shaping", but for this to happen there must be effective and coherent communication between executive and representative functions and the structures to facilitate this communication (Johnson and Hatter, 2004: 13). At present, the balance of power between the centrally-appointed manager and the locally-elected councillors is weighted too much in the manager's favour.

THE ROLE OF COUNCILLORS

Given this context, further questions arise about the role of elected councillors in local decision-making processes and their relationship with the citizens that elect them. First, Ireland is unusual in that the distance between elected councillors and the citizens is substantially greater than any other Member State of the EU with the exception of Britain (see Tables 4 and 5 for more detail). Jones and Stewart (1993: 15) contend that "a greater number of members embeds local government into the grassroots. They make local government more responsive to the local community and understanding of its wishes and needs". It has been argued that it is neither unusual nor unreasonable to see fewer councillors than one might expect because so many functions normally allocated to local government in other countries are within the remit of other public agencies in Ireland. We suggest that this latter point, though of value at one level, misses the importance of local councillors and their role in enabling and sustaining local democracy.

Elected councillors, chosen through the ballot box, are our civic leaders. They derive authority from us through the electoral process, and they are essential to our understanding of representative democracy. However there are new challenges to their civic authority and to the publicly-perceived legitimacy of locally-elected councillors. First, is the challenge to their democratic mandate. This is shown most clearly in declining voter turnout. Second, there is an argument that elected representatives need to be as diverse as the populations they represent if democracy is to thrive. This is not to suggest that local councillors can only speak for those who share a similar background, identity or experience. However, a failure to reflect diversity is likely to reduce the quality and variety of debate and to reduce legitimacy in the eyes of constituents. This leads us to conclude that in order to develop a more democratic form of local government, or rather, successfully embed democracy in our system of local governance, we need to recognise the centrality of elected councillors to local democracy.

On a more positive note, there is anecdotal evidence that this situation is changing as the new generation of councillors from all political parties are focused on making their political impact at local level. This appears to be a direct outcome of the implementation of the Local Government Act 2001 which prohibits councillors from holding Dáil seats.

Table 4: Council, Councillor and Citizen Relationships in the European Union

Country	Population	Number of Relevant Local Councils	Average Population per Council	Average Size of Council	Population per Elected Councillor
France	59.6 million	36,700	1,600	14	118
Austria	8.2 million	2,350	3,500	17	209
Sweden	8.8 million	310	28,400	111*	256
Germany	83 million	15,300	5,400	15	350
Finland	5.2 million	452	11,500	28	410
Italy	57.7 million	8,100	7,100	12	608
Spain	40 million	8,100	4,900	8	610
Belgium	10.3 million	589	17,500	22	811
Greece	10.6 million	1033	10,300	10	1,075
Denmark	5.4 million	275	19,600	17	1,115
Portugal	10.1 million	308	32,800	29	1,131
Netherlands	16 million	548	29,000	19	1,555
Ireland	3.8 million	118	33,000	14	2,336
United Kingdom	59.6 million	468	127,350	49	2,603

Source: Knox, 2002: 5.   * Includes deputies, elected at the same time.

Table 5: Local Government Electors per Councillor in Britain and Ireland

Country	Number of Councillors	Population	Number of Councils	Average Population per Council	Population per Elected Councillor	Local Government Electors per Councillor
Northern Ireland	582	1.7 million	26	64,980	2,903	2,059
Scotland	1,245	5.1 million	32	153,000	4,108	3,201
Wales	1,273	2.9 million	22	128,000	2,314	1,761
Ireland	1,627	3.9 million	118	33,000	2.336	1,654

Source: Knox, 2002: 3

THE ROLE OF CIVIL SOCIETY

Finally, we argue that there has been a growing effort to involve civil society in local decision-making processes. This is partly a result of a central government focus on developing forms of active citizenship and partly a result of Ireland's experience of social partnership. For example, in city and county councils, trade unions, chambers of commerce, local community and voluntary sector organisations have been invited to join Strategic Policy Committees to work with councillors in developing locally-appropriate policies and in City/County Development Boards (CDBs) civil society representatives form a significant cohort.

One of the most important innovations in recent years for community groups has been the establishment of community fora by CDBs. In general, the community fora are open to groups working in various capacities within communities in each area. Since their inception, community fora have become the main vehicle through which members of community and voluntary groups are nominated to Strategic Policy Committees, CDBs and other local government sub-committees. Area partnerships, local drugs taskforces and RAPID/CLÁR structures tend to have similar forum-type structures in their specific areas.

Outside of the community fora, community groups and individuals can influence the local decision-making processes through attending the 'clinic' of their local TD, who can in turn contact their local councillor. They can also contact the councillor directly, although this causes much more difficulty in a city such as Dublin than it does for a town council such as Balbriggan. In addition, most local governments provide opportunities for consultation with their communities, groups and individuals, on major issues: the five yearly County/City Development Plan are an example of one such opportunity.

Overall, we found that there is a willingness on the part of local government officials to encourage wider community participation in local governance, even if the mechanisms are not always in place to ensure the widest possible represen-tation of the community. In this context, Ireland has been very slow to devise and implement complementary forms of participation such as citizens' juries. Despite this reluctance, the inclusion of the community and voluntary sectors on the CDBs has facilitated an input by these sectors into the overall strategy and framework for future developments relative to their areas.

A PLURALIST AND DEMOCRATIC FUTURE?

However, with the establishment of structures to facilitate the involvement of social partners and the statutory agencies, a major question remains over whether this represents the development of a more pluralist decision-making process and, if it does, whether this new pluralism represents a step towards a more democratic and accountable form of decision making. Arguably, while more people are involved in the decision making process, the process itself has become less transparent and accountable to the public as a variety of local public agencies negotiate their own relationships with each other and central government while at the same time diluting the influence of elected councillors. Furthermore, the structures that have been established often appear to be devised in such a way as their use depends on whether local governments decide the "circumstances are propitious" (Forde, 2004: 62). Once again this reflects the "managerialist" emphasis in Irish local government (Sullivan, 2001: 17).

The experience of local governance and local democracy in Ireland

n the previous sections of this paper we have shown that the last twenty years have seen the establishment of a number of new public and quasi-public agencies at local level in Ireland. Some commentators have referred to the early 1990s as the era of a "new localism in Irish public policy" (Walsh et al., 1998: 18). Furthermore, while the impact of these agencies on local governance processes is as yet unclear, the establishment of area partnerships, community partnerships, city/county enterprise boards, LEADER+ groups and city/county development boards has significantly increased the number of people perceived to be participating in the local governance process. While these new agencies have varying aims and objectives, it is possible to identify a common characteristic: there is an emphasis on the development of partnerships between the public, private and third sectors, which arguably mirrors the model of social partnership pioneered at national level. At one level, it could be said that this system is more democratic than the structure which previously existed, given that there is now a more diverse composition of the membership of new agencies and organisations, but at the same time and as we have already shown, it is widely accepted that locally-elected officials in Ireland have more limited powers than their equivalents in other countries (Quinn, 2004: 452-455; John, 2001: 25). While Adshead suggests that the establishment of these new agencies incorporates "an ever wider circle of policy actors into sub-national government" and helped recast local governments as "central co-ordinators for the ever-widening arena of actors in sub-national development" (2003: 119), in essence, this has resulted in the appearance of more stakeholders and institutional actors but no perceptible actual increase in legitimate public scrutiny. In this section we assess the evidence.

NEW STAKEHOLDERS IN GOVERNANCE

As noted earlier, Ireland lacks an effective and coherent regional tier of governance, while at the level of city and county there has been a significant growth in the number of local public agencies (see Table 6 for a brief synopsis of the main local and regional public agencies operating in Ireland and Appendix II for greater detail). At first glance, the evidence suggests a large increase in the number of stakeholders participating in local public policy formulation. Despite the lack of "any formal institutional reorganisation of sub-national government, over time the need to develop policy delivery mechanisms led to the creation of several types of organisation operating at sub-national level" (Adshead, 2003: 118). Some of these perform the functions undertaken by regional and local administrations in other countries (see Table 1 for more detail). Almost all are national organisations with regional offices. For example, some services, such as income maintenance programmes are administered by local offices of central government departments; others such as the supply of gas or electricity are the responsibility of appointed boards; and some such as the health service and aspects of the local education system are run by single-purpose bodies which contain indirect representation from local government. Most of these latter do not have regional autonomy.

The system of central control of local functions is effective in many ways. However, when it comes to dealing with local issues and difficulties, national government in most cases is unable to respond in a manner that is both appropriate and useful. Moreover, Chubb observes that the consequence of the creation of this "jungle of administrative areas" is that it "is both impenetrable to the ordinary citizen and frequently inconvenient for any type of business that involves more than one authority or organisation" (1992: 263). Thus, it is important to note that:

(a) Ireland is a very centralised state where a wide range of services delivered at local level are managed and planned by national organisations with little or no local or regional autonomy;

(b) as a result Ireland allocates a very small proportion of government expenditure to locally accountable public agencies;

(c) of these locally-accountable public agencies, it is estimated that local governments are responsible for approximately 90 per cent of locally-controlled and scrutinised public expenditure;

(d) the role of central government remains the same and if anything may have been strengthened by the lack of a coherent template for establishing the new agencies.

CITY/COUNTY DEVELOPMENT BOARDS

Taking the role of the City/County Development Boards as an example. At first glance they appear to provide an excellent mechanism to devise local policy priorities in a managed and deliberate manner. However, key agencies involved in the structures, such as Enterprise Ireland, FÁS and the IDA, are national organisations with little or no local autonomy. As a result the ability of their nominees to sign up to a locally-agreed strategy is severely limited. Furthermore, key service providers, such as the Department of Education and Science, are not represented on the Boards, limiting the ability of the CDBs to implement agreed strategies in areas which fall under the remit of the Department in question. In essence, it is relatively more straightforward to sign off on the strategy than it is to ensure that agencies comply with its provisions, particularly as the CDBs have no power of sanction.

That being said CDBs have carried out innovative work and have provided a mechanism for local councillors and communities, via their community forums, to engage in policy discussions with local public agencies in way that was not possible before the CDBs' establishment. In addition, some CDBs have provided mechanisms to include other stakeholders in the local policy-formulation process. For example, Fingal Development Board provides a position for the Institute of Technology in Blanchardstown and Dublin City University on its Board.

Despite these positive aspects, it is clear that CDBs are overly reliant on influence as opposed to statutory sanction to ensure their organisational objectives are met. In addition, members of CDBs have been unable to commit their agencies to CDB strategies and actions and have been unable to influence the planning processes of major public agencies.

A point made in most of the relevant policy and academic literature is that a local governance process is interactive because no single agency - public, quasi-public or private – has the knowledge and resource capacity to tackle the problems unilaterally. We find that this principle has not been taken on board and as a result attempts to provide an appropriate institutional architecture for local governance have been flawed. For example, the recent report of the 'Lyons Inquiry into Local Government' in Britain has recommended that local government's "lead role in convening partners" should be formally recognised "by the introduction of a statutory duty to co-operate" with local government (Lyons, 2006: 10).

FINANCING LOCAL GOVERNMENT

In this context it is important to grasp the weak position of local government in Ireland vis-à-vis its counterparts in the EU, in particular its ability to act in an autonomous manner. Local governments in Ireland are unusual in that they are responsible for spending such a small percentage of national income in the various services they provide. For example, expenditure by Irish local governments in 2001 was €5,872 million. This represented approximately 6 per cent of GNP. This was broken down into €2,665 million for day-to-day revenue current expenditure and €3,207 million for capital expenditure (Dollard, 2003: 325). In terms of its revenue sources, Ireland is also unusual in that its local governments are quite limited in their ability to raise revenue (Tables 7, 8 and 9 provide more detail). Neil Collins notes the "loss of domestic rates as a truly independent local tax had a marked effect on the morale of managers and councils". The most visible symbol of local autonomy, setting the rate level, was thus removed" (1987: 48). A point generally accepted in the rest of the EU and the USA, which is that some power of local taxation is essential for local government to retain some degree of autonomy, remains unacceptable in Ireland. This absence of capacity for independent action constrains local governments from, for example, introducing a 'statutory duty to cooperate' with them, which would allow them to take a lead role in convening partners.

Broadly it can be said that Irish local government financing has progressed through three key stages:

(a) where a significant proportion of local government revenue was generated through local mechanisms, in this cases domestic rates;

(b) where an attempt was made to generate revenue through local service charges; and

(c) the current situation where the introduction of the Local Government Fund in the late 1990s has meant the return in importance to a centralised funding system.

Table 6: Local and Regional Public Agencies in Ireland
(*see Appendix II for more detail*)

Organisation and number	Type (Decision-making and/or Advisory)	Composition of Board
1. County Councils (29)	Decision making	Elected Councillors and the County Manager.
2. City Councils (5)	Decision making	Elected Councillors and the City Manager.
3. Town Councils (75)	Decision making	Elected Councillors
4. Borough Councils (5)	Decision making	Elected Councillors
5. Regional Assemblies (2)	Advisory	City and County Councillors from the constituent local governments.
6. Regional Authorities (8)	Advisory	City and County Councillors from the constituent local governments.
7. Regional Health Authorities (4)	Decision making	The composition of the HSE Regional Boards has not yet been clarified.
8. Rural Tourism Development Boards (7)	Decision making	Chairperson and board members appointed by Fáilte Ireland
9. Regional Fisheries Boards (7)	Decision making	Mixture of Ministerial nominations, tourism representatives, local councillors and representatives of the numerous fishing organisations.
10. Regional Drugs Task Forces (10)	Advisory	The RDTFs include representatives from the following organisations: Regional Drug Co-coordinator of the Health Service Executive, local government; VEC; Department of Education and Science; Department of Community, Rural and Gaeltacht Affairs; Garda Siochána, Probation and Welfare Services; FÁS; Revenue Commissioners; Social Partners.
11. Harbour Authorities (5)	Decision making	Representatives of local government, harbour users, chambers of commerce and ministerial appointments

12. Port Companies (12)	Decision making	Worker representatives from the company, representatives of relevant local government, and individuals appointed by Minister.
13. City/County Development Boards (34)	Advisory	Typical composition is as follows: Representatives of local government (7), local development (6), state agencies (9) and Social Partners (6-8).
14. City/County Enterprise Boards (35)	Decision making	Typical composition is as follows: independent chairperson, members from the local government (4), nominees of state agencies, Social Partners, (10)
15. Area partnerships (38)	Decision making	Typical composition is as follows: independent chairperson, members from the local government (3-6), nominees of state agencies (6), Social Partners (6), and local community (6).
16. Community partnerships (33)	Decision making	Typical composition is as follows: independent chairperson, members from the local government (3-6), nominees of state agencies (6), Social Partners (6) and local community (6).
17. LEADER (35)	Decision making	Typical composition is as follows: independent chairperson, members from the local government, nominees of state agencies, Social Partners and local community.
18. County/City Childcare Committees (33)	Decision making	Typical composition is as follows: providers' nominees, members from the local government, nominees of state agencies, Social Partners and local community.
19. Vocational Education Committees (33)	Decision-making	Typical composition is as follows: chief executive, members from the local government, nominees from teaching unions and parents.

20. Local Drug Task Forces (18)	Advisory	Typical composition is as follows: nominees of state agencies and local community.
21. RAPID (45)	Advisory	Typical composition is as follows: members of local government, members of the Local Area Partnership, members of the Local Drug Task Force and local community. Each programme also has a co-ordinator who is employed by the relevant local government.
22. CLÁR (18)	Advisory	Typical composition is as follows: members of local government, members of the Local Area Partnership, members of the Local Drug Task Force and local community. Each programme also has a co-ordinator who is employed by the relevant local government.

Table 7: Local Governments Revenue Expenditure 1981-2002

Programme	1981		2002	
Housing and building	€236	28%	€499	16%
Road transportation and safety	€241	29%	€920	30%
Water supply and sewerage	€112	13%	€350	11%
Development incentives and controls	€19	2%	€149	5%
Environmental protection	€77	9%	€557	18%
Recreation and amenity	€46	6%	€272	9%
Agriculture, education, health and welfare	€55	7%	€180	6%
Miscellaneous	€47	6%	€172	5%
Total	€833	100%	€3,099	100%

Source: Department of Environment, Heritage and Local Government Returns of Local Taxation and Local Authority Estimates (cited by Dollard, 2003: 326)

Table 8: Breakdown of Local Government Income Receipts
1977-2002*

Revenue Source	1977	1981	1991	2002
Rates	34%	12%	21%	24%
Government grants	46%	65%	61%	47%
Other	20%	23%	18%	29%
	100%	100%	100%	100%

* The figures in this table are indicative and not directly comparable due to changes in accounting practices over the years.

Source: Department of Environment, Heritage and Local Government Returns of Local Taxation and Local Authority Estimates (cited by Dollard, 2003: 328)

If we compare Irish practice with the standards set out for the protection and democratic freedom of local government in the Council of Europe's European Charter for Local Self-Government 1985, of which Ireland is a signatory, we can see important divergences from what are considered best practice. For example the Charter stipulates that:

(a) local governments must have adequate financial resources of their own (Article 9);
(b) central government must not undermine local governments' powers by administrative action (Articles 4 and 8);
(c) local governments must be able to determine their own taxes (Article 9).

Ireland has made some progress in addressing other aspects of the Charter. For example, the Local Government Act 1991 provided for local governments in Ireland to have a power of general competence (Article 4) and Ireland has provided for constitutional recognition for local governments (Article 2). However, it is important to note the situation with regard to local government income and expenditure in Ireland. As Table 8 shows, on average almost 50 per cent of a local government's income takes the form of a direct grant from central government. This on its own is not problematic, many systems of local government financing involve at least some form of central government, often for equalisation purposes. What is of concern is the rigidity and inflexibility of the remaining finance-raising methods.

Table 9: Main Local Taxes in the EU Member States

Country	1st tier	2nd tier	3rd tier
Austria	Property tax Municipal business tax		
Belgium	Additional property tax Additional income tax Additional vehicle tax	Additional property tax General provincial tax (Flanders)	
Cyprus	Business tax Property tax Tax on hotels		
Czech Republic	Property tax Visitor tax Tax on cultural events Tax on gambling		
Denmark	Local income tax Property tax	Local income tax Property tax	
Estonia	Property tax Sales tax Vehicle tax Advertising tax		
Finland	Local income tax Property tax		
France	Residence tax Property tax Business tax Household waste disposal tax	Residence tax Property tax Business tax Property transfer duties	Property tax Business tax Tax on vehicle registration

Germany	Property tax		
	Business tax		
Greece	Tax for street cleaning and electrification		
	Property tax		
	Tax on use of electricity		
Hungary	Residence tax		
	Property tax		
	Business tax		
	Tourism tax		
Ireland*	**Property tax (on businesses)**	**Property tax (on businesses)**	
Italy	Property tax	Additional income tax	Regional business tax
	Additional income tax	Tax on public space occupation	Additional income tax
	Tax on public space occupation	Vehicle tax	
	Household waste disposal tax		
Latvia	Property tax		
Lithuania	Property tax		
	Tax on rented land		
Luxembourg	Property tax		
	Municipal business tax		
Malta	N/A		
Netherlands	Property tax		
	Tourism tax	Additional vehicle tax	
Poland	Property tax		
	Inheritance tax		
	Civil register tax		
	Tax on agricultural activities		
Portugal	Property tax		
	Tax on real estate transactions		
	Additional corporate income tax		
	Municipal vehicle tax		

Slovakia	Property tax		
	Tax on hotels		
	Sales tax on alcohol and tobacco		
	Advertising tax		
Slovenia	Property tax		
	Tax on real estate transactions		
	Visitor tax		
	Tax on donations		
	Tax on gambling		
Spain	Property tax	Additional business tax	Income tax
	Local business tax		Inheritance tax
	Local vehicle tax		Property transfer
	Construction tax		duties
	Urban area capital		Wealth tax
	gains tax		
Sweden	Local income tax	Local income tax	
United Kingdom	Property tax	Property tax	Additional Income tax (Scotland)

Source: Dexia, 2004: 51

*   In Ireland's case the three tiers are taken to refer to town councils (1st tier), county
     and city councils (2nd tier) and regional authorities (3rd tier).

The implications for local democracy in Ireland

The local public decision-making process in Ireland can be summed up as follows:

(a) the vast majority of public expenditure decisions are made at *national* level;

(b) local governments are responsible for the vast majority of public expenditure decisions at *local* level;

(c) local governments in Ireland have a drastically reduced set of functions in comparison to their European counterparts;

(d) elected public representatives play a much reduced role in the policy-formulation and decision-making processes than their European counterparts;

(e) the ability of citizens to influence both the policy-formulation and decision-making processes beyond casting their ballot is quite narrow.[1]

While some commentators suggest that Irish local government may be suffering from reform fatigue (Keogan and Callanan, 2005: 502), we suggest that the reform process to date reflects a "silo mentality" and very little attention has been paid to examining the potential for developing a coherent and more democratic local governance process. We contend that Irish citizens want to see "institutions on offer that they can control or influence" and that these institutions "control things that they care about" (Stoker, 2006: 9). In contrast to the attempts by the Irish state to reform its local public agencies, a comprehensive review of local and regional governance has taken place in Northern Ireland. The review was launched in June 2002 and central to the Northern Ireland Executive's Review of Public Administration (RPANI) was a willingness to openly ask questions about agencies' rationale, value for money and their relationship to the public. Ireland has never carried out a similar exercise yet there are many lessons we can learn from the experience of the RPANI. Two in particular stand out: the RPANI's focus on the local governance process as opposed to local government reform and the detailed examination of the role of councillors as civic leaders, including their relationship to the citizens and communities they represent and their input into the local public policy decision-making processes. As this study shows the role of councillors in Ireland is very constrained in relation to their European counterparts (Quinn, 2004: 452-455; John, 2001: 25). Until the Irish state engages in a similar review of its local public decision-making processes any proposed reform of local democracy in Ireland is likely to be piecemeal and could make what is a bad situation even worse.

In conclusion, there are usually three reasons given for having a robust system of local government. First, as multi-purpose bodies, local governments are able to co-ordinate the provision of several services within a corporate framework: in the Irish context this is not necessarily the case as local governments in Ireland have a very narrow range of competencies in comparison to their EU counterparts. Second, the independent element introduced by both local elections and a separate basis of taxation allows local governments to develop policies that reflect the needs and aspirations of local populations: as we have seen Irish local governments are particularly constrained in their ability to raise finance and act autonomously. Finally, local government has also been justified in terms of wider political values.

Among the foremost of these is the promotion of liberty by the dispersal of power from the centre to the localities. No one would argue that local government always acts fairly or that central government is always autocratic. The argument is simply that of pluralism: when there are several centres of power, disagreements are likely to come into the open and open government is preferable to the coteries of centralism. This paper concludes that Ireland's system of local governance falls behind on all three criteria.

Notes

1   The main policy document drafted by local governments in Ireland is the county/city development plans. In essence these are zoning exercises that, once accepted, set the framework for spatial planning and development for a five year period. In the majority of cases the relevant authorities facilitate a substantial consultation exercise and engage with as many stakeholders (interest groups, communities etc.) as feasible. Once the plan is voted on by the councillors it is accepted. However, the consultation exercises often lack a broad deliberative component and effectively encourage groups to make submissions on issues of local rather that county or city-wide importance. On the other hand the legal system provides many communities and individuals with the ability to overturn decisions. As a result we have developed a system where it is very hard to say yes to any proposal and significantly easier to block a proposal.

Bibliography

1. Adshead, Maura (2003) 'Policy networks and sub-national government' in Maura Adshead and Michelle Millar (eds) *Public administration and public policy in Ireland*, London: Routledge.
2. Barrington Report (1991) *Local government reorganisation and reform – report of the advisory expert committee*, Dublin: Government Publications.
3. Byrne, Paula (2003) 'Urbanisation' in Mark Callanan and Justin Keogan (eds) *Local Government in Ireland – Inside Out*, Dublin: Institute of Public Administration.
4. Callanan, Mark (2003a) 'The role of local government' in Mark Callanan and Justin Keogan (eds) *Local Government in Ireland – Inside Out*, Dublin: Institute of Public Administration.
5. Callanan, Mark (2003b) 'Local government and the European Union' in Mark Callanan and Justin Keogan (eds) *Local Government in Ireland – Inside Out*, Dublin: Institute of Public Administration.
6. Castells, Manuel (2002) 'Local and global: cities in the network society' in Journal of Economic and Social Geography 93 (5) 548-58
7. Chubb, Basil (1992) *The government and politics of Ireland*, London: Longman.
8. Clarke, Susan (2003) 'Globalisation and cities: a North American perspective' in Robin Hambleton, Hank Savitch and Murray Stewart (eds) *Globalisation and local democracy – challenge and change in Europe and North America*, Basingstoke: Palgrave Macmillan.
9. Collins, Neil (1987) *Local government managers at work*,

Dublin: Institute of Public Administration.

10. Coughlan, Maurice and Donal de Buitleir (1996) *Local government finance in Ireland*, Dublin: Institute of Public Administration.

11. Denters, Bas and Len Rose (2005) *Comparing local governance: trends and developments*, London: Palgrave.

12. Dexia (2004) *Local finance in the twenty five countries of the European Union*, Paris: Dexia Editions.

13. Dollard, Gerard (2003) 'Local government finance: the policy context' in Mark Callanan and Justin Keogan (eds) *Local Government in Ireland – Inside Out*, Dublin: Institute of Public Administration.

14. Forde, Ciaran (2004) 'Local government reform in Ireland 1996-2004: a critical analysis' in *Administration* Volume 52, Number 3, pp. 57-72.

15. Gaffikin, Frank and Mike Morrissey (1999) 'Understanding the contemporary city' in Frank Gaffikin and Mike Morrissey (eds) *City visions – imagining place, enfranchising people,* London: Pluto.

16. Giddens, Anthony (2000) 'The Globalizing of Modernity', in David Held and Anthony McGrew, (eds) *The Global Transformations Reader*, London: Polity Press.

17. Hines, Colin (2000): *Localization: A Global Manifesto*, Earthscan.

18. Hoffman, Gerry (2006) 'Size, Shape and Sustainability: Local Government Reform in Queensland, Australia' in *Economic Development* Issue 92/93, pp. 6-10.

19. John, Peter (2001) *Local governance in Western Europe.* London: Sage.

20. Johnson, Ken and William Hatter (2004) *Realising the Potential of Scrutiny: Research and Recommendations on the Overview and Scrutiny function in Local Government.* London: New Local Government Network/The Centre for Public Scrutiny.

21. Jones, Gerry and John Stewart (1993) 'When the numbers don't add up to democracy' *Local Government Chronicle* 8th January: 15.

22. Kavanagh, Adrian (2004) 'The Local Elections in the Republic of Ireland' in *Irish Political Studies*, Volume 19, Number 2, pp. 64-84.

23. Keogan, Justin and Mark Callanan (2003) 'The future' in Mark Callanan and Justin Keogan (eds) *Local Government in Ireland – Inside Out*, Dublin: Institute of Public Administration.

24. Knox, Colin (2002) 'Local government representation' a briefing paper for the Review of Public Administration Northern Ireland.

25. Kooiman, Jan (1993) 'Social-political governance: Introduction' in Jan Kooiman (ed) *Modern governance – new government society interactions*, London: Sage.

26. Kooiman, Jan (2003) *Governing as governance.* London: Sage.

27. Lyons Inquiry into Local Government. 2006. *National Prosperity, local choice and civic engagement: A new partnership between central and local government for the 21st century*, Norwich: HMSO.

28. Munck, Ronaldo (2003) *Reinventing the city? Liverpool in comparative perspective*, Liverpool: Liverpool University Press.

29. Munck, Ronaldo (2005) *Globalisation and social exclusion: a transformationalist perspective*, Bloomfield: Kumarian Press.

30. Office of the Deputy Prime Minister (2006) *All Our Futures: The challenges for local governance in 2015*, Wetherby: ODPM Publications.

31. Quinn, Brid (2004) 'Irish local government in a comparative context' in Mark Callanan and Justin Keogan (eds) *Local Government in Ireland – Inside Out*, Dublin: Institute of Public Administration.

32. Savitch, Hank (2003) 'The globalisation process' in Robin Hambleton, Hank Savitch and Murray Stewart (eds) *Globalisation and local democracy – challenge and change in Europe and North America*, Basingstoke: Palgrave Macmillan.

33. Stoker, Gerry (2006) *What is local government for? Refocusing*

local governance to meet the challenges of the 21st century.
London: New Local Government Network.

34. Sullivan, Helen (2001) 'Modernisation, democratisation and community governance' in *Local Government Studies*, Volume 27, Number 3, pp.1-24.

35. Tierney, John (2006) 'The Importance of the Local in a Global Context', in David Jacobson, Peadar Kirby and Deiric Ó Broin (eds) *Taming the Tiger: Social Exclusion in a Globalised Ireland*, Dublin: Tasc at New Island.

36. Walsh, Jim, Sarah Craig and Des McCafferty (1998) *Local Partnerships for Social Inclusion*, Dublin: Oak Tree.

Appendix I

Structure and functions of local and regional public agencies

NAME OF AGENCY	TYPE	FUNCTIONS & RATIONALE	NO. & SIZE OF BOARDS	COMPOSITION OF BOARD	APPOINTMENT, ELECTION & DISMISSAL
COUNTY COUNCILS	SERVICE & POLICY	Functions divided into 8 programme groups (1) Housing & Building (2) Roads & Transportation (3) Water & Sewerage (4) Environmental Protection (5) Recreation (6) Agriculture, Education, Health & Welfare (7) Planning (8) Misc. Services.	There are 29 County Councils with between 20 and 48 members. The amount of councillors that can be elected depends on the population of the county/city e.g. Cork has 48 members whereas Carlow only has 21.	Elected Councillors & the County Manager. Reserved Functions are the functions of the elected members. All other functions are called Executive Functions and are carried out by the County Manager.	Councillors are elected every 5 years by the public. Election is open to those 18 & over and excludes Ministers/Ministers of State/MEP's/Chairperson of the Dail & Seanad/Oireachtas Select Committees/TDs & Senators. Manager position filled by Local Appointments Commission. Position is contract based for 7 year term. Cathaoirleach/Chairperson is elected annually by the council members
CITY COUNCILS	SERVICE & POLICY	Functions divided into 8 programme groups (1) Housing & Building (2) Roads & Transportation (3) Water & Sewerage (4) Environmental Protection (5) Recreation (6) Agriculture, Education, Health & Welfare (7) Planning (8) Misc. Services	There are 5 city councils: Cork (31 members), Dublin (52), Galway (15), Limerick (17) & Waterford (15).	Elected Councillors & the City Manager. Reserved Functions are the functions of the elected members. All other functions are called Executive Functions and are carried out by the City Manager.	Councillors are elected every 5 years by the public. Election is open to those 18 & over and excludes Ministers/Ministers of State/MEP's/Chairperson of the Dail & Seanad/Oireachtas Select Committees/TDs & Senators. Manager position filled by Local Appointments Commission. Position is contract based for 7 year term. Lord Mayor is elected on an annual basis by city council members.
TOWN COUNCILS	SERVICE & POLICY	Housing, roads, waters supply, sewerage, planning: for certain operations under these programme the parent county council is responsible (see Callanan, 2003, p50). According to Callanan, town councils have similar functions to county/city councils but increasingly tend to devolve their main functions upwards to county level.	75 town councils in total, 72 of which have 9 members. The other 3 town councils have 12 members	Elected Councillors & Mayor/Chairperson.	Councillors are elected every 5 years by the public. Election is open to those 18 & over and excludes Ministers/Ministers of State/MEP's/Chairperson of the Dail & Seanad/Oireachtas Select Committees/TDs & Senators Manager position filled by Local Appointments Commission Position is contract based, for 7 year term. Cathaoirleach/Mayor is elected annually by the council members
BOROUGH COUNCILS	SERVICE & POLICY	Housing, roads, waters supply, sewerage, planning: for certain operations under these programme the parent county council is responsible (see Callanan, 2003, p50). According to Callanan, town councils have similar functions to county/city councils but increasingly tend to devolve their main functions upwards to county level.	5 in total; Clonmel, Drogheda, Kilkenny, Sligo & Wexford, each with 12 members.	Publicly elected Councillors plus the Mayor/Chairperson.	Councillors are elected every 5 years by the public. Election is open to those 18 & over and excludes Ministers/Ministers of State/MEP's/Chairperson of the Dail & Seanad/Oireachtas Select Committees/TDs & Senators Manager position filled by Local Appointments Commission Position is contract based, for 7 year term. Cathaoirleach/Mayor is elected annually by the council members

NAME OF AGENCY	TYPE	FUNCTIONS & RATIONALE	NO. & SIZE OF BOARDS	COMPOSITION OF BOARD	APPOINTMENT, ELECTION & DISMISSAL
REGIONAL ASSEMBLIES	SERVICE	Promote co-ordination of provision of public services in all their areas. Monitor the impact of all EU programmes for assistance under the Community Support Framework. They are also responsible for managing Regional Programmes of the National Development Plan.	2 boards with 70 members in total. (1) Border-Midland-Western Regional Assembly (29 members) and (2) South & Eastern Regional Assembly (41 members) Full committee meets 6 times annually, whilst sub-committees meet quarterly. The EU Regional Operational Monitoring Committee meets bi-annually.	City & County Councillors. Each Regional Assembly has its own CEO & full time administrative staff who are funded both by the county/city councils and for part of their work by the Dept. of Justice, Equality and Law Reform.	Appointed by their constituent county/city councillors. Must be a member of a county or city council & relevant Regional Authority.
REGIONAL AUTHORITIES	SERVICE & ADVISORY	To prepare and implement the Regional Planning Guidelines as set out in the Planning & Development Act of 2000. Promote the co-ordination of public service provision. Also involved on the monitoring committee overseeing the implementation of the EU Structural funds in their area. This role is an advisory one as the Regional Assemblies hold overall responsibility for monitoring these funds.	8 in total. Operate in Dublin (29 members); South East (35 members); Mid-West (26 members); South West (23 members); Mid-West (26 members); Border (37 members); Midlands (23 members); Mid East (21 members)	City & County Councillors from the constituent local authorities.	Members are all county/city councillors appointed by the local Authority. The number of persons to be appointed to be members by each constituent local authority ranges from 14 in the case of Dublin City Council to 5 each from some of the smaller counties. Amount of seats that a Local Authority has on its Regional Authority is (loosely) dependent on the population under the local authority's jurisdiction. Other conditions of appointment include tenure, disqualification, resignation, casual vacancies, attendance at meetings.
REGIONAL HEALTH AUTHORITIES	SERVICE & POLICY	4 Health Service Executive Regions (HSE) are currently being set up by the Dept. of Tanaiste, Health & Children to provide & administer health care & service in Ireland via the hospitals, care centres, treatment programmes, GP's etc.	4 HSE Regions are in the process of being set up. These will be called the Dublin/North Leinster Region, the Dublin/South Leinster Region, the Southern Region and the Western Region. Details on membership and format of these boards has not yet been confirmed. At present there are 9 Health Board Regions in operation, each with its own board of directors, CEO and administration staff.	The composition of the HSE Regional Boards has not yet been clarified by the Dept. of the Tanaiste, Health & Children. The National Health Service Executive has a board consisting of 9 board members and one Chairperson drawn mainly from the private sector, health sector and the Universities.	The composition of the HSE Regional Boards has not yet been clarified by the Dept. of the Tanaiste, Health & Children.
REGIONAL TOURISM DEVELOPMENT BOARDS	SERVICE	Ensure that tourism actives are carried out effectively at regional & local level. Prepare a tourism development plan for the region.	5 in total. Each region is serviced by a Tourism Authority.	Chairperson and Board members are appointed by Fáilte Ireland. The Boards are usually composed of representatives of local tourism interests and local government.	Various positions in the Regional Tourism boards are advertised both internally and in the National Press.

NAME OF AGENCY	TYPE	FUNCTIONS & RATIONALE	NO. & SIZE OF BOARDS	COMPOSITION OF BOARD	APPOINTMENT, ELECTION & DISMISSAL
REGIONAL FISHERIES BOARDS	SERVICE	Responsible for fisheries management in their region. Improving environmental quality, developing & protecting the fisheries resource in their respective regions.	7 Boards in total ranging in size from 19 members for the Eastern Region to 26 members for the Southern Region.	Mixture of Ministerial nominations, tourism representatives, local councillors and representatives of the numerous fishing organisations throughout the country.	There are a number of appointments made directly by the Minister of Communications, Marine & Natural Resources. These range from 4 appointments on the Eastern Region Board to 8 in the Shannon, Western & North Western regions. These nominations are made in consultation with the Central Fisheries Board. Various fishing organisations often hold internal elections to decide who will be nominated to their relevant fisheries board.
REGIONAL DRUGS TASK FORCES	POLICY & ADVISORY	Conduct research & maintain database to establish the extent, nature & pattern of drug misuse in their respective regions. Develop regional plans for their area to address gaps in service provision.	10 in total.	The RDTFs include representations from the following organisations: Regional Drug Co-co-ordinator of the Health Board; Local Authority Representation; VEC; Health Board, Dept. of Ed. & Science; Dept. of Community, Rural & Gaeltacht Affairs, Garda Síochána; Probation & Welfare Services; FAS; Revenue Commissioners; Voluntary/Community Sector; Area Based Partnerships	Chairperson and members are appointed by the Minister
HARBOUR AUTHORITIES	SERVICE	Responsibility for the operation and maintenance of their harbours under the Harbours Act 1946 to 2000. However, the Minister exercises controlling powers in the areas of finance/appointment of certain officers/fixing of certain harbour rates/disposal of property etc.	5 in total: Castletownbere, Dunmore East, Howth, Killybegs, Rossaveel. All other harbours were placed back in the control of their respective county councils.	Includes representatives of users of the harbours, local authorities, commercial, interests, chambers of commerce and ministerial representation.	Elected in the year local elections are held. Some members are appointed by the Dept. of Communications, Marine & Natural Resources.
PORT COMPANIES	SERVICE	Responsible for management & development of main commercial ports under the Harbours Act. 1946 - 2000. Obliged to conduct business in a cost effective and self sufficient manner.	12 boards - Arklow, Cork, Drogheda, Dublin, Dundalk, Dun Laoghaire, Foynes, Galway, New Ross, Shannon, Waterford, Wicklow.	Board of Directors consists of representatives of employees of company, relevant local authority, some individuals appointed by ministerial appointment.	Minister appoints one or more persons after consultation with the Chamber of Commerce.
CITY/COUNTY DEVELOPMENT BOARDS	POLICY	Avoid duplication in delivery of services at local level. Adopted 10year city/county strategies for economic, social & cultural development in 2002. Aim to bring a more coherent delivery of services by state agencies at local level. Aim to combat social exclusion & promote local development.	34 in total. One for every city/county council area.	Typical composition is as follows: Local Government (7) Local Development (6) State Agencies (9) & Social Partners (6)	Nominations can be broken down for each sector as follows: Local Government: Mayor, County/City Manager, Council Representative (1) and Chairpersons of SPC's. Local Development: CEBs (2) ABPCs (2) Leader Groups (2) State Agencies: FAS,I.D.A.,Enterprise Ireland,V.E.C.,Western Development Commission, Dept. of Family & Social Affairs,Udaras na Gaeltachta,Garda Síochána, Health Boards & Teagasc. Social Partners: Employer & Business organisations (1), Agriculture & Farming (1) Trade Unions (1) and members of the community &

NAME OF AGENCY	TYPE	FUNCTIONS & RATIONALE	NO. & SIZE OF BOARDS	COMPOSITION OF BOARD	APPOINTMENT, ELECTION & DISMISSAL
CITY/COUNTY ENTERPRISE BOARDS	SERVICE & POLICY	Promote micro-enterprise at local level, i.e. business with 10 or less employees. They are given clear enterprise and job creation objectives with responsibility for business areas not already covered by the State's industrial development agencies.	35 in total; 4 in Dublin & Cork, 2 in Limerick & Tipperary. Made up of 14 board members	Consists of independent chairperson (usually city/county manager or private sector/community person) 4 members are from the city/county council, the other 10 are nominees of state agencies, social partners, promoters of small business etc. Each CEB has a CEO.	4 Members are publicly elected officials whilst the remainder are nominated by various social partners such as trade unions etc as well as local small business representatives.
AREA PARTNERSHIPS	SERVICE	Prepare and implement a local development plan to counter disadvantage in their area. Remit widened to increase their emphasis on social inclusion. Involved in the promotion of enterprise, education and community development.	38 in total. There are usually between 20-30 board members on each partnership board.	Involves state agencies, social partners, local elected members, community & voluntary sector.	As Partnership Companies are companies limited by guarantee the board of each partnership is subject to the rules and regulations set down by the appropriate companies legislation.
COMMUNITY PARTNERSHIPS	SERVICE	Targets disadvantage in such areas as long term unemployment, discrimination against travellers, the disabled & women; ethnic minorities, old people & the homeless; ethnic minorities, ex prisoners & offenders etc etc.	33 in total. Average board size is 25 members.	Involves state agencies, social partners, local elected members, community & voluntary sector.	As Partnership Companies are companies limited by guarantee the board of each partnership is subject to the rules and regulations set down by the appropriate companies legislation.

NAME OF AGENCY	TYPE	FUNCTIONS & RATIONALE	NO. & SIZE OF BOARDS	COMPOSITION OF BOARD	APPOINTMENT, ELECTION & DISMISSAL
LEADER GROUPS	SERVICE	7 key services: Technical support for rural development, Craft, Enterprises & Local Services, Training & Recruitment Assistance, Exploitation of local produce, Environmental protection, Rural Tourism, Transnational/Inter-territorial co-operation.	Originally 16 programmes under LEADER 1 from 1992-1994. Increased to 37 groups from 1995-2000 and currently 35 (22+13) groups up until 2006.	Representatives of local community, state agencies, local authorities & social partners.	Board members can only serve for a maximum of 6 years and must be re-nominated and re-elected after their 3rd year.
CITY & COUNTY CHILDCARE COMMITTEES	SERVICE	Aim to advance the quality of childcare services through implementation of 5 year CCC Childcare Strategy. To implement at local level the government's co-ordinated strategy to develop quality childcare in Ireland	33 in total. Operate in each city and county area.	A typical membership would comprise of a Childcare would comprise of approx. 16 members as follows: Statutory Agencies-Fás (1), Health Boards (2), Dept. of Social & Family Affairs (1), local VEC (1), City/County Development Board (1). National Voluntary Childcare Organisations - IPPA (1), ISPCC(1), NCNA(1). Parents-Community & Private (2). Childcare Provider-Community & Private (2). Social Partners-Chamber of Commerce (1),Community Forum (1), ICTU (1). Local Development-Local Area Partnerships (2). Equality & Diversity-Representative (1)	The Childcare Committee is elected on an annual basis. It is preferable that people appointed to the committee remain in their seat for the entire term of The committee, however it is not uncommon for larger organisations to rotate the people who fill their seat on the committee. Nominated every council election year.
VOCATIONAL EDUCATION COMMITTEES	SERVICE & POLICY	Manage and develop education in their area through vocational schools, community colleges, PLC courses, adult education and back to school schemes.	33 in total. 5 VEC in city council areas, 28 county VECs. Dublin has three separate VECs; Dublin City, Dun Laoghaire/Rathdown and Co. Dublin VEC (which covers both South County Dublin and Fingal County)	Each VEC has a CEO. Members from relevant city/county council; representatives of staff of the VEC & parents etc.	

NAME OF AGENCY	TYPE	FUNCTIONS & RATIONALE	NO. & SIZE OF BOARDS	COMPOSITION OF BOARD	APPOINTMENT, ELECTION & DISMISSAL
INTEGRATED AREA PLAN STRUCTURES	SERVICE	To improve both the physical environment and the socio-economic landscape of the targeted area through the implementation of an agreed masterplan.	49 IAPs currently in operation throughout the country.	Board is comprised of representatives from: Local Authority, Chamber of Commerce, Trade Council, Representatives of Historical & Architectural Conservation Interests, Community Representatives, Social Partners, Partnership Companies, Development Agencies.	Members of the IAP are appointed through the relevant county/city council and for the duration of the IAP project.
LOCAL DRUG TASK FORCES	SERVICE & POLICY	Development of community based initiatives to link in with existing programmes being run by statutory agencies. Helps local communities & voluntary organisations to participate in the planning, design and delivery of services including advice & support centres, community drug teams, training, awareness and rehabilitation schemes etc etc.	18 LDTFs in total. 14 LDTF areas in Dublin Cork & Bray as well as four other urban areas (Limerick, Waterford, Carlow and Galway)	Board members drawn from statutory, voluntary & community sectors.	Statutory members usually come from Dept. of Justice, Equality & Law Refrom; Dept. of Tanaiste, Health & Children, Dept of Education & Science. Voluntary sector members are drawn from organisations dealing with drug abuse in the locality. Community is represented by community reps drawn from local community forum.
RAPID PROGRAMMES	SERVICE	Strand 1 targets 25 Urban centres with the greatest concentration of disadvantage for priority funding under the NDP. Strand 2 targets 20 provincial towns in a similar fashion. The programme is also about facilitating closer co-ordination and better integration in the delivery of local services.	25 urban centres targeted as part of RAPID 1 programme & 20 provincial towns targeted as part of RAPID 2 programme.	Each programme is implemented by an AIT (Area Implementation Team) which comprises of representatives from all or some of the following: Health Boards, Local Authority, VEC, Dept. of Social & Family Affairs, FAS, Local Partnerships, Local Residents & LDTF. Each programme also has a co-ordinator who is employed by the local authority	Programmes usually run on a 3 year term after which a new AIT is formed if needed.
CLAR PROGRAMMES	SERVICE	Set up to complement both RAPID 1 & RAPID 2. CLAR provides funding & co-funding to Government Dept., state agencies and local authorities in accelerating investment in selected priority developments.	Works within 18 different counties including all of county Lietrim.	Each programme is implemented by an AIT (Area Implementation Team) which comprises of representatives from all or some of the following: Health Boards, Local Authority, VEC, Dept. of Social & Family Affairs, FAS, Local Partnerships, Local Residents & LDTF. Each programme also has a co-ordinator who is employed by the local authority	Programmes usually run on a 3 year term afterwhich a new AIT is formed if needed.

NAME OF AGENCY	GEOGRAPHICAL AREA SERVED	FINANCE/SOURCES & EXPENDITURE	ACCOUNTABILITY
COUNTY COUNCILS	Boundary is set by the geographical area of their county with the exception of the area served by a city council if one exists within their county. The area traditionally referred to as County Dublin is also an exception as it was divided into 3 subregions as part of the Local Government Act 1993: South County Dublin, Dun Laoghaire/Rathdown and County Fingal. Dublin City is one of 5 city councils.	2 elements to funding: Current & Capital. Current includes: (1) State Grants (2) Charges for services (3) Commercial Rates (4) Local government fund. Capital includes (1) State Grants (2) Borrowings (3) Receipt of sales of capital assets such as housing & land.	Members & staff of County Councils are accountable in three primary ways; electoral, managerial and financial. Staff of the council are accountable to both the councillors themselves and the Dept. of the Environment, Heritage & Local Governmnet (DEHLG). Financially, the council is accountable to both the Comptroller & Auditor General (C&A.G.) and the DEHLG and County Managers can be removed if two-thirds of elected members vote for resolution for removal.
CITY COUNCILS	5 city areas of Cork, Dublin, Galway, Limerick and Waterford.	2 elements to funding: Current & Capital. Current includes: (1) State Grants (2) Charges for services (3) Commercial Rates (4) Local government fund. Capital includes (1) State Grants (2) Borrowings (3) Receipt of sales of capital assets such as housing & land.	Members & staff of City Councils are accountable in three primary ways; electoral, managerial and financial. Staff of the council are accountable to both the councillors themselves and the DEHLG. Financially the council is accountable to both the C&A.G. and the DEHLG and City Managers can be removed if two-thirds of elected members vote for resolution for removal.
TOWN COUNCILS	Areas formerly served by Urban District Councils.	Obtain financing from county council by means of annual demand.	Members & staff of Town Councils are accountable in three primary ways; electoral, managerial and financial. Staff of the council are accountable to both the councillors themselves and the DEHLG. Financially the council is accountable to both the C&A.G. and the DEHLG. Under 2001Act, town council may by resolution apply to the minister to dissolve the town council.
BOROUGH COUNCILS	There are 5 Borough Councils situated in Clonmel, Drogheda, Kilkenny, Sligo & Wexford.	Obtain financing from county council by means of annual demand.	Members & staff of Borough Councils are accountable in three primary ways; electoral, managerial and financial. Staff of the council are accountable to both the councillors themselves and the DEHLG. Financially the council is accountable to both the C&AG and the DEHLG. Under 2001Act, town council may by resolution apply to the minister to dissolve the town council.

NAME OF AGENCY	GEOGRAPHICAL AREA SERVED	FINANCE/SOURCES & EXPENDITURE	ACCOUNTABILITY
REGIONAL ASSEMBLIES	There are 2 Regional Assemblies; the Boarder/Midlands/Western (BMW) Assembly and the Southern & Eastern Assembly. The BMW Region is made up of 13 counties: Cavan, Donegal, Galway, Laois, Leitrim, Longford, Louth, Mayo, Monaghan, Offaly, Roscommon, Sligo, Westmeath. The Southern & Eastern Region consists of the counties within the 5 Regional Authority areas of: Dublin, South Eastern, South Western, Mid Western & Mid Eastern.	Most funding comes from the constituent county/city councils. Some funding is made available through EU Structural Funds & National Exchequer Funds (through the Dept. of Finance). For example, the managing & auditing of the EU regional operational programme, which is carried out by the staff of the assembly is 75% EU funded and 25% funded by the Dept. of Finance. The funding for available to the BMW Region was estimated at €4,094million (2003) whilst the Southern & Eastern Region received €5,378.72million.	Staff are recruited and promoted from the local government pool of the public service through the DEHLG. However, their wages are part funded by the Dept. of Finance and staff are also accountable to the elected representatives on the assembly. Assembly members themselves are elected public representatives and as such are accountable to the electorate as well as to the DEHLG.
REGIONAL AUTHORITIES	Boarder = Donegal, Leitrim, Sligo, Cavan, Monaghan, Louth. Dublin = County & City Dublin. Mid-East = Meath, Kildare, Wicklow. South-Eastern = Wexford, Carlow, Kilkenny, Waterford, Tipperary South. South-Western = Cork, Kerry. Mid West = Limerick,Clare,Tipp. North West = Mayo, Roscommon, Galway Midlands = Longford, Offaly, Laois, Westmeath	Financing of activities of Regional Authorities is largely borne by the constituent Local Authorities. Additional financial assistance is given under the NDP towards the Regional Authority's EU related functions	County Councillors are accountable to both their constituents and to the Dept. of the Environment, Heritage and Local Government. Full time staff of the Regional Authority are primarily accountable to the board of the authority which meets at least once a month but also to the Regional Manager who is selected from among the city/county managers of the constituent councils of the region.
REGIONAL HEALTH AUTHORITIES	The 4 HSE Regions are divided as follows: (1) Western Region = Clare, Donegal, Galway, Limerick, Mayo, North Tipperary, Roscommon, Sligo & Leitrim. (2) Southern Region = Carlow, Kilkenny, Nort Lee, North Cork, Kerry, South Lee, South Tipperary, Wexford, Waterford & West Cork. (3) Dublin/North-Leinster = Cavan, Monaghan, Louth, Meath & North Dublin. (4) Dublin/Mid-Leinster = Kildare, West Wicklow, Laois, Offaly, Longford, Westmeath, South Dublin & Wicklow.	The HSE relies primarily on funding by the Irish Exchequer which is administered by the Dept. of Health & Children.	The 4 HSE Regions will be accountable to a National HSE which in turn is accountable to the Dept. of the Tanaiste, Health & Children.
REGIONAL TOURISM DEVELOPMENT BOARDS	5 Regions; South-West, South-East, West, Nort-West, Midlands-East.	Finance received from various sources including Failte Ireland; the tourism industry, local authorities and funds from commercial activities.	Regions receive approx. one third of their funding from Failte Ireland which is a semi state organisation responsible for promoting tourism within the Republic. PwC (PriceWaterhouseCoopers) is currently compiling a report on behalf of the Government into the structure of tourism in Ireland. Indications suggest that there may be a restructuring along the lines of those implemented in the Health sector.

NAME OF AGENCY	GEOGRAPHICAL AREA SERVED	FINANCE/SOURCES & EXPENDITURE	ACCOUNTABILITY
REGIONAL FISHERIES BOARDS	There are 7 regions: Eastern, Southern, South-Western, Shannon, Western, North Western, Northern. The regions are drawn up on a catchment basis.	Funding is made available by the Dept. of Communications, Marine & Natural Resources.	Under the aegis of the Dept. of Communications, Marine & Natural Resources. Accounts audited by C &A.G.
REGIONAL DRUGS TASK FORCES	Based in the 10 regional health board regions.	Funding is made available by the Dept. of Community, Rural & Gaeltacht Affairs.	Under the aegis of the Dept. of Community, Rural and Gaeltacht Affairs.
HARBOUR AUTHORITIES	Harbours divided into 2 subsections. (A) Harbours with some commercial traffic (B) Harbours with little or no commercial traffic.	Dept. of Communications, the Marine and Natural Resources. Harbours now under the auspices of county/city councils are run from levies placed on users of the harbour, although grants can be obtained from the Dept. in times of emergency, i.e. damage caused by severe storms etc.	Under the aegis of the Dept. of Communications, Marine & Natural Resources.
PORT COMPANIES	New Ross, Waterford, Dundalk, Cork, Drogheda, Dublin, Dun Laoghaire, Shannon/Foynes, Galway, Wicklow, Arklow.	Most monies come from the business created by the port itself.	Under the aegis of Dept. of Communications, Marine & Natural Resources. Minister has the power to establish further companies in respect of harbours
CITY/COUNTY DEVELOPMENT BOARDS	One development board for every county/city council area.	Core costs are drawn on from the relevant county/city council, i.e. salaries for administrative staff and costs of meetings etc. There have been moves, however, for agencies involved in the Development Board (e.g. IDA or Leader or Local business groups) to contribute to the running of the board, either through monetary means or in kind. Also, major projects that relate to specific areas of development, for example tourism, often receive donations from the agencies who are most likely to benefit from the project.	Process overseen by an inter-departmental taskforce chaired by the Minister of the Environment.

NAME OF AGENCY	GEOGRAPHICAL AREA SERVED	FINANCE/SOURCES & EXPENDITURE	ACCOUNTABILITY
CITY/COUNTY ENTERPRISE BOARDS	Usually one per county except in the cases of Dublin, Cork, Limerick and Tipperary.	City & County Enterprise Boards are funded by the Irish Government and part financed by the European Union under the National Development Plan 2000-2006. Financed by the Exchequer & EU Structural Funds. Had a budget of £25.4 million in 1999. €190.4million was allocated for the period 2000-2006.	Dept. of Enterprise responsible for overall co-ordination & supervision of CEB. Accounts are audited by C &A.G.
AREA PARTNERSHIPS	Partnership Companies are set up in designated disadvantaged areas. There are counties with no partnership companies whilst others have many e.g. Dublin City and Counties have a total of 11 partnerships whilst there are 18 rural based partnerships throughout the country.	Funding made available through Area Development Management Ltd as part of the Local Development Social Inclusion Scheme which in turn is funded by the NDP (2000-2006)	Under the aegis of Dept. of Community, Rural and Family Affairs. Local Plans evaluated by ADM Ltd. Structure mirrors social partnership arrangement at national level with feedback links expected between Directors of local partnerships and parent organisations. Local Partnerships are independent companies limited by guarantee with a board of directors and as such are subject to the same audits etc that apply to any other limited company.
COMMUNITY PARTNERSHIPS	Same principle as Area Partnerships only focused on specific communities.	Funding made available through Area Development Management Ltd as part of the Local Development Social Inclusion Scheme which in turn is funded by the NDP (2000-2006)	Under the aegis of Dept. of Community, Rural and Family Affairs. Local Plans evaluated by ADM Ltd.

NAME OF AGENCY	GEOGRAPHICAL AREA SERVED	FINANCE/SOURCES & EXPENDITURE	ACCOUNTABILITY
LEADER GROUPS	Initially 16 targeted areas but now one in every county.	Initially funded by the European Union, until 2000 when it became publicly funded by the government through the Dept. of Agriculture & Food. Leader programme currently divided into two programmes: (1) LEADER Plus Programme with a public contribution of €73.7million is in place in 22 areas throughout the country. (2) The LEADER National Rural Development Programme is set up to complement LEADER Plus and is funded by public money totalling €75.6million. It covers the 13 areas not covered by LEADER Plus.	LEADER was initially under the direction of Dept. of Agriculture and Food until 2002. LEADER is now under the aegis of Dept. of Community, Rural and Family Affairs. Local business plans are agreed between local action groups and the Dept.
CITY & COUNTY CHILDCARE COMMITTEES	There is a Childcare Committee to every county/city council area.	Supported by the ESF and Exchequer funding under the Equal Opportunities Childcare Programme 2000-2006	Dept. of Justice, Equality and Law Reform is responsible for the EOCP 2000-2006 which in turn is administered by ADM Ltd. The Dept. set up the National Co-ordinating Committee which in turn oversees the work of the various city/county childcare committees.
VOCATIONAL EDUCATION COMMITTEES	One in each County/City Council Area with the exception of Dublin which has 3 VEC's covering its 4 council areas.	Funded mainly from the State. In the 2005 estimates, received £735,383 (an increase of 5% over 2004 estimates).	Department of Education Minister has power to make regulations governing procedures of VEC. VEC holds meetings at least once a month except in July & September. AGM help before December 1st. Inspector from Dept. of Education is entitled to be present at public meetings.

NAME OF AGENCY	GEOGRAPHICAL AREA SERVED	FINANCE/SOURCES & EXPENDITURE	ACCOUNTABILITY
INTEGRATED AREA PLAN STRUCTURES	In operation in parts of Dublin, Limerick, Galway & Waterford as well as smaller towns throughout the country since 2000.	Money made available through the National Development Plan 2000-2006. Total of €158million invested over the 7 years, €110.5million to the South & Eastern Region and €47.5million to the BMW Region. Also Grant assistance of €16million in 2004 bringing total grant assistance up to €58.194million. Further provision of €21million for 2005.	Plans are drawn up by the city/county council in partnership with local partners & local communities. Annual report on progress of IAP submitted each March 1st.
LOCAL DRUG TASK FORCES	Ballyfermot, Ballymun, Blanchardstown, Bray, Canal Communities, Clondalkin, Dublin N.E., Cork, Dublin 12, Dun Laoghaire/Rathdown, Finglas/Cabra, North Inner City, South Inner City & Tallaght.	Since 2001, the LDTFs have been funded by the Exchequer through the Cabinet Committee on Social Inclusion. In this time, over £14million euro has been allocated on an annual cost basis.	Under the aegis of Dept. of Community, Rural and Gaeltacht Affairs. Funds are administered through ADM Ltd.
RAPID PROGRAMMES	RAPID Strand 1 covers the following areas: Dublin North, Ballymun, Finglas, North Inner City 1 & 2, South West Inner City 1 & 2, Pearse Street Area, South County Dublin, Tallaght, North County Dublin, Dun Laoghaire/Rathdown & parts of Cork, Waterford, Limerick & Louth. Strand 2 covers the towns of Athy, Ballinasloe, Carric-on-Suir, Cavan, Longford, Mallow, New Ross, Tipperary, Tuam & Youghal.	Funding comes from Europe through the National Development Plan.	ADM Ltd manages the RAPID Programme on behalf of the Dept. of Community, Rural & Gaeltacht Affairs. A National Monitoring Committee oversees the operation of Stand 1 & 2 of the RAPID Programme. There is also a National Co-ordinator who liases with the individual co-ordinators.
CLAR PROGRAMMES	Parts of counties: Cavan, Clare, Cork, Donegal, Galway, Kerry, Limerick, Longford, Louth, Mayo, Meath, Monaghan, Roscommon, Sligo, Tipperary, Waterford, Westmeath and all of county Lietrim.	Funding comes from Europe through the National Development Plan.	Under the aegis of the Dept. of Communications, the Marine & National Resources.

NAME OF AGENCY	PROVISION FOR COMMUNITY CONSULTATION	PARTNERSHIPS & JOINT WORKING	ESTABLISHED
COUNTY COUNCILS	Provision for community consultation is made in a number of ways; through the holding of clinics and also through community representation on sub structures of the city/county council such as Strategic Policy Committees etc. Not less than one third of SPCs are made up of sectoral interests. According to the Institute of Public Administration (IPA) Review of SPCs published in 2004, an average of 34% of these sectoral interests came from the Community/Voluntary sector.	Some members of the council hold seats on regional boards of tourism, health, education & development as well as SPCs, various committees dealing with drug abuse, planning, the environment etc. and the Area Partnerships. The councils also come into contact with several groups through the varied membership of the SPCs.	Forms of Local Government in Ireland can be traced back to 19th Century statutes by the British Government. The most current and up to date definition is outlined in the Local Government Act of 2001.
CITY COUNCILS	Community provision is made in a number of ways; through the holding of clinics and also through community representation on sub structures of the city/county council such as Strategic Policy Committees etc. Not less than one third of SPCs are made up of sectoral interests. According to the IPA Review of SPCs published in 2004, an average of 34% of these sectoral interests came from the Community/Voluntary sector.	Some members of the council hold seats on regional boards of tourism, health, education & development as well as SPCs, various committees dealing with drug abuse, planning, the environment etc. and the Area Partnerships. The councils also come into contact with several groups through the varied membership of the SPCs.	Forms of Local Government in Ireland can be traced back to 19th Century statutes by the British Government. The most current and up to date definition is outlined in the Local Government Act of 2001.
TOWN COUNCILS	Community provision is made in a number of ways; through the holding of clinics and also through community representation on sub structures of the city/county council such as SPCs etc. Not less than one third of Municipal Policy Committees are made up of sectoral interests. According to the IPA Review of SPCs published in 2004, an average of 34% of these sectoral interests came from the Community/Voluntary sector.	Some members of the council hold seats on regional boards of tourism, health, education & development as well as Municipal Policy Committees, various committees dealing with drug abuse, planning, the environment etc. and the Area Partnerships.	Forms of Local Government in Ireland can be traced back to 19th Century statutes by the British Government. The most current and up to date definition is outlined in the Local Government Act of 2001.
BOROUGH COUNCILS	Community provision is made in a number of ways; through the holding of clinics and also through community representation on sub structures of the city/county council such as SPCs, Area Partnerships, etc. Not less than one third of Municipal Policy Committees are made up of sectoral interests. According to the IPA Review of SPCs published in 2004, an average of 34% of these sectoral interests came from the Community/Voluntary sector.	Some members of the council hold seats on regional boards of tourism, health, education & development as well as MPCs, various committees dealing with drug abuse, planning, the environment etc. and the Area Partnerships.	Forms of Local Government in Ireland can be traced back to 19th Century statutes by the British Government. The most current and up to date definition is outlined in the Local Government Act of 2001.

NAME OF AGENCY	PROVISION FOR COMMUNITY CONSULTATION	PARTNERSHIPS & JOINT WORKING	ESTABLISHED
REGIONAL ASSEMBLIES	Assembly members are directly elected members of local government and as such represent the people of their respective city/county.	As monitors of European and NDP programmes, the regional assemblies have much contact with a wide range of bodies.	Intially proposed in 1998 as a way of retaining EU Objective 1 designation for the counties of the western seaboard. Established formally in 1999 by the Minister of the Environment, Heritage and Local Government.
REGIONAL AUTHORITIES	Members of the Regional Authority are council members directly elected by the citizens of their respective counties/cities.	Regional Authorities work in partnership with all relevant development bodies in the area. For example, local County Development Boards (CDB), the Industrial Development Authority (IDA), Enterprise Ireland and public bodies such as the tourist board, the Garda and An Post.	Regional Authorities have their origins in the 1991 Local Government Act and came into being through the Regional Authorities Establishment Order 1993 (SI No. 394 of 1993)
REGIONAL HEALTH AUTHORITIES	Exact details on the make-up of the 4 Regional HSE structures has not yet been fully clarified by the Dept. of the Tánaiste, Health & Children.	Exact details on the make-up of the 4 Regional HSE structures has not yet been fully clarified by the Dept. of the Tánaiste, Health & Children.	The HSE took control of administering the health system in January 2005 having been announced as part of the Dept. of Health and Children's Health Service Reform Programme 2003.
REGIONAL TOURISM DEVELOPMENT BOARDS	Exact details for community consultation are unavailable due as Rural Tourism Development Boards were only established mid 2006.	The Tourism Boards work in partnership with the relevant County/City Councils as well as with any Arts/Cultural groups, boards or committees in the Area. Through their National organisation Fáilte Ireland, they also have some contact with Tourism Ireland, the all-island tourism board.	Boards were established in 2006 to replace the Regional Tourist Authorities which were established in 1964

NAME OF AGENCY	PROVISION FOR COMMUNITY CONSULTATION	PARTNERSHIPS & JOINT WORKING	ESTABLISHED
REGIONAL FISHERIES BOARDS	There is no official community representation on the fisheries board except the presence of elected local councillors.	The fishery boards are not involved in any major partnership or joint working agreements.	Central Fisheries Board was established 1980.
REGIONAL DRUGS TASK FORCES	Details are not yet available	No details available.	Set up as part of the key recommendations of the National Drugs Strategy 2001-2008.
HARBOUR AUTHORITIES	Community provision is through the elected members of council who sit on the board and through the representation of the Chambers of Commerce representative.	Apart from dealings with the Dept. of Communications, Marine & Natural Resources, the Harbour Authorities also work in partnership with the DEHLG.	Established as part of the Harbours Act 1946.
PORT COMPANIES	Community provision is through the elected members of council who sit on the board and through the representation of the Chambers of Commerce representative.	Apart from dealings with the Dept. of Comm., the Marine & the Natural Environment, the Harbour Authorities also work in partnership with the DEHLG.	Established as part of the Harbours Act 1946.
CITY/COUNTY DEVELOPMENT BOARDS	Consultation with local community & voluntary organisations. Plans made available through local authority. Various local authority committees feed into development board's work on issues such as rural transport initiatives, tourism in the area, youth affairs & promotion of the Irish language.	Development Boards work in close partnership with local businesses, local educational centres and development agencies such as the IDA.	Recommended by the Task Force on the Integration of Local Government & Local Development Systems (August 1998) and began functioning in 2000.

NAME OF AGENCY	PROVISION FOR COMMUNITY CONSULTATION	PARTNERSHIPS & JOINT WORKING	ESTABLISHED
CITY/COUNTY ENTERPRISE BOARDS	The four city/council representatives are publicly elected officials. Other community provision comes in the form of the representative of local business.	Enterprise Boards work in close partnership with development agencies and small business agencies such as Irish Small & Medium Enterprise Association (ISME) and local chambers of commerce.	Established in 1993 by the Dept. of Enterprise, Trade and Employment.
AREA PARTNERSHIPS	One of the primary focuses of the partnership process is social inclusion so there is an emphasis on participation by the community/voluntary/ sector. In principle, partnership companies should be located, owned and run by the local community in designated disadvantaged areas.	By their very nature, partnership companies and agencies are a joint working of various organisations and agencies ranging from state bodies to social partners and community/voluntary sector organisations.	Established by the Government in 1991 under the Programme for Economic & Social Progress. Initially 12 set up between 1991-1993. Extended to 38 from 1994-1999 and continued at that number from 2000-2006.
COMMUNITY PARTNERSHIPS	One of the primary focuses of the partnership process is social inclusion so there is an emphasis on participation by the community/voluntary/sector. In principle, partnership companies should be located, owned and run by the local community in designated disadvantaged areas.	By their very nature, partnership companies and agencies are a joint working of various organisations and agencies ranging from state bodies to social partners, community/voluntary sector organisations and elected representatives such as councillors and in some cases TDs.	Established by the Government in 1991 under the Programme for Economic & Social Progress. Initially 12 set up between 1991-1993. Extended to 38 from 1994-1999 and continued at that number from 2000-2006.

NAME OF AGENCY	PROVISION FOR COMMUNITY CONSULTATION	PARTNERSHIPS & JOINT WORKING	ESTABLISHED
LEADER GROUPS	LEADER programmes are mainly rural based and as such cannot function without the participation of the community action groups it is set up to work with.	LEADER groups work in partnership with local rural organisations such as the ICA, Macra na Feirme, the IFA etc as well as development organisations at county level as LEADER should not duplicate or replace The work down by such bodies as the CDB or CEB.	LEADER 1 was began in 1992 and was succeeded by LEADER 2 in 1994 in Europe and began in May 1995 in Ireland.
CITY & COUNTY CHILDCARE COMMITTEES	There members of the community/voluntary sector on the childcare committee along with various publicly elected officials.	In February 2003, a formal link was established between CCC & CDB The CCC also works with the Dept. of Health, the Dept. of Justice (who have ultimate responsibility for the national childcare programme), the Dept. of Education and various service and education providers to the childcare sector.	The CCC were initiated in 2002 and are run under the EOCP 2006.
VOCATIONAL EDUCATION COMMITTEES	Community provision is made firstly through the elected councillors who sit on the board and secondly through the parents representatives who sit on the board.	IVEA (Irish Vocational Education Association) which represents he 33 VECs at national level is a nominating body to the Seanad, the National Council for Curriculum & Assessment, the National Council for Educational Awards, the Council of CERT among others.	The Vocational Education Committees were set up and established through the Vocational Act 1930 and its subsequent amendments.

NAME OF AGENCY	PROVISION FOR COMMUNITY CONSULTATION	PARTNERSHIPS & JOINT WORKING	ESTABLISHED
INTEGRATED AREA PLAN STRUCTURES	Cross-sectoral monitoring committee with representation from local commercial & community groups and will have overall responsibility for monitoring the IAPs progress in achieving their outlined objectives.	IAPs are effectively sub structures of the city/county council and as such have the same set of partnerships and joint working.	Established in 1999 as part of the second phase of the Urban Renewal Scheme of the same year.
LOCAL DRUG TASK FORCES	Community reps are local residents who work in local organisations. These organisations meet together under the umbrella of a community forum and elect representatives to the LDTFs.	LDTFs work closely with the Garda Siochána, Community Gardái, the Health boards (especially drug clinics) and staff from the Justice Dept.	The LDTFs were established in 1997 with Bray being added in 2000.
RAPID PROGRAMMES	RAPID is a community run organisation in essence. To insure this is the case there is an SIM Group set up within the relevant CDB as well a National Monitoring Group which is an interdepartmental group under a chairperson.	Through their work, AITs consult with a range of public bodies such as LDTF's, the Garda etc.	Launched under the NDP in February 2001.
CLÁR PROGRAMMES	CLÁR is a community run organisation in essence. To insure this is the case there is an SIM Group set up within the relevant CDB as well a National Monitoring Group which is an interdepartmental group under a chairperson.	Through their work, AITs consult with a range of public bodies such as rural interest groups, the Garda etc.	It was introduced in October 2001 under a commitment by the PPF to target disadvantaged rural areas.

What formal provisions exist which would allow local citizens to influence the decision-making process of different agencies?

COUNTY/CITY COUNCILS

The primary method by which the community can influence the decision-making process of County/City Councils is through exercising their preference in local elections. The residents of the area, using the electoral system of proportional representation, directly elect all council members. Approval or dissatisfaction with the councils can be shown through exercising the right to vote at local elections. These elections are held every 5 years. During the working term of the council, most elected members of the council hold private consultations with constituents at public venues throughout their constituency. At these 'clinics,' local residents have the opportunity to discuss issues with the council members in private. Clinics are commonly held in a local hall or in a meeting room in a hotel or public house. However, there is no formal provision or requirement for councillors to hold clinics and their prevalence varies widely between councillors.

Information concerning services provided by local government such as housing, planning, maintenance etc. are broadly advertised in the media and at public buildings.

Objections and appeals can be made formally to the council and are often investigated by independent committees.

BOROUGH/TOWN COUNCILS

Borough and Town councils function in much the same way as city/county councils, albeit on a smaller scale. However, borough and town councils have tended to devolve many of their powers upwards to the city/county level and, accordingly, provision for community consultation and influence usually rests with the relevant city/county council.

REGIONAL ASSEMBLIES

The membership of the two Regional Assemblies comprises county/city councillors. There are no formal structures for community involvement in decision making at this level. Community representation, therefore, lies with the relevant councillors who sit on the assembly on behalf of their council and its constituents.

REGIONAL AUTHORITIES

As with the Regional Assemblies, membership is made up of elected city/county councillors who make representations on behalf of their constituency and its inhabitants.

REGIONAL HEALTH EXECUTIVES

The health service is currently in the throes of major restructuring. As part of this process, the current 11 regional health boards are to be replaced by 4 HSE regions. At present, the community is represented on health boards by a mixture of elected representatives from the relevant councils and local people involved in various organisations concerned with public health, such as LDTF representatives and local disability groups etc. There have been concerns, particularly from local governments, that the centralisation of the regions will diminish the influence of publicly elected officials but overall plans for board membership have not been completely finalised.

REGIONAL TOURISM DEVELOPMENT BOARDS

The Regional Tourism Development Boards (RTDB) were recently established as successors to the Regional Tourism Boards. Chairpersons were appointed by Fáilte Ireland in late August 2006. The primary function of the RTDBs is to direct the formulation and regular review of a comprehensive tourism development strategy for its region, to cover all key aspects of tourism development including the product, enterprise support, training, marketing, infrastructure and environmental management needs of tourism in the region. At present the boards are composed of representatives of local government and tourism interests within the region. Policies regarding provisions for community consultation are still being formulated.

REGIONAL DRUGS TASK FORCES (RDTF)

The RDTFs, which will carry out strategic research and planning on behalf of the Local Drugs Task Forces, have only recently come into operation. Policies regarding provision for community consultation are still being formulated.

HARBOUR AUTHORITIES AND PORT COMPANIES

There are no formal provisions for community engagement within the Harbour Authorities and Port Companies, with membership usually restricted to those involved in that area of business. However, the government does appoint local councillors to the board and many of the business interests are locally focused, such as local fishermen etc.

CITY/COUNTY DEVELOPMENT BOARDS (CDB)

The composition of the board of a development board is made up of representatives from local government, state agencies and the social partners. Included in the Social Partners strand are members from the community and voluntary sector, the former being drawn from the community forum structures that exist within each county. The composition of CDBs is regulated in the Local Government Act 2001, Part 13, Section 129(3) and also in the document: "A Shared Vision for County/City Development Boards" which was published by the Department of the Environment, Heritage and Local Government in May 2000.

CITY/COUNTY ENTERPRISE BOARDS (CEB)

Similarly to the CDBs, there is provision made on the boards of CEBs for the inclusion of the social partners. As part of this agreement, there must be at least 2 representatives of community groups on the boards of the CEB. However, the selection of these representatives need not come from the local community forum. There is also representation from local councillors on the CEB and this is another method through which the community can influence the work of the CEB.

AREA PARTNERSHIPS

Area partnership companies have a relatively strong track record when it comes to community participation. As their funds are administered by ADM Limited, the companies are required to have community representatives on their board. The number varies depending on the size of the partnership area but the average nationwide is 6 community representatives on each board. Often these representatives are drawn from the official community forum structure but sometimes the partnerships will approach groups individually if they feel that the local community forum does not adequately represent groups from disadvantaged areas, which are their primary concern.

COMMUNITY PARTNERSHIPS

Even more so than Area Partnerships, Community Partnerships, by their very nature, involve a high participation rate of the local community. Although some community partnerships are quite large in size (there are now urban community partnerships that are bigger than some rural based area partnerships), in general, community partnerships tend to be relatively small in size and therefore involve a lot of community input.

LEADER

LEADER groups, due to the rural nature of their work, rely heavily on gaining the active participation of a wide group from the community. County Dublin Rural LEADER for example has representatives on its board from the relevant community forums in Fingal, Dún Laoghaire/Rathdown and South Dublin. In addition, there is representation from two youth groups and a rural women's network. There is also a full time community development officer, reflecting the bottom-up ethos of the LEADER programme in general.

CITY AND COUNTY CHILDCARE COMMITTEES

The City and County Childcare Committees, which operate in each of the county/city districts, are administered by ADM Limited and are ultimately accountable to the Department of Justice, Equality and Law Reform which stipulates that each committee must have representation from the community, nominated by the relevant community forum. The various parent representatives who also sit on the boards of the childcare committees also represent the community.

VOCATIONAL EDUCATION COMMITTEES (VEC)

The boards of the VECs were recently reconstituted as part of the Vocational Education Committee (Amendment) Act 2001. In Part 2 Section 8, the Act provides for community representation through the appointment of 4 persons to the board who are nominated by the council, in consultation with staff and pupil representatives, from a wide cross section of the community. Applications are invited for nomination through the relevant press under the following guidelines: students, trustees of community colleges maintained by the VEC, members of the staff of the VEC, voluntary/community organisations, Irish-language interests, persons partaking in trades, professions, commercial/industrial activities within the VEC area.

LOCAL DRUGS TASK FORCES (LDTF)

The Local Drugs Task Forces work under the aegis of the Department of Community, Rural and Gaeltacht Affairs. All LDTFs are required by the department to have community representatives sitting on their boards. Community representatives should be local residents of the area who are members of the relevant community forum through their participation in local organisations/groups. LDTF policies affecting the wider community are conveyed to the community through the representative who shares this information with the community forum.

RAPID PROGRAMMES

Both RAPID programmes, Strands 1 and 2, are community focused in their ethos. Funding for the RAPID programmes is administered by ADM Ltd and, as such, is subject to Social Inclusion Monitoring reports. As part of this process, a paper was commissioned by ADM Ltd on community participation in which the local residents were identified as the 'primary stakeholders' in the project. It also suggests that RAPID-specific community forums be set up in which representatives of the community could get to know the relevant agencies at work in their area. Despite these measures, RAPID has been criticised for its poor levels of community involvement and the lack of transparency in selecting local participants in its Area Implementation Teams.

CLÁR PROGRAMMES

CLÁR is the sister programme of RAPID. Its target areas are based in rural areas, many in the west and south west of the country. As with RAPID, there is a high emphasis on community participation and the programme is subject to SIM reports from the Department of Community, Rural and Gaeltacht Affairs.

List of interviewees and discussants

Professor Ronnie Munck	-	Dublin City University
Professor Peadar Kirby	-	Dublin City University
Dr. Brendan Williams	-	UCD
Sheena McCambley	-	Ballymun Regeneration Limited
Brian Carty	-	PLANET (Area Partnerships Network)
Cllr. Mary Murphy	-	Dublin City Council
Cllr. Liam Kelly	-	Dublin City Council
Chris O'Malley	-	Ballymun Partnership
Cllr. Anne Devitt	-	Fingal County Council
Ciarán Staunton	-	Fingal Development Board
Michael Cowman	-	Centre for Cross-Border Community Development, Dundalk Institute of Technology
Brendan Bartley	-	NUI Maynooth
Odran Reid	-	Northside Partnership
Marian Vickers	-	Northside Partnership
Dr. Mark Callanan	-	Institute of Public Administration
Catherine Murphy TD	-	Dáil Éireann
Caoimhin Ó Tuathail	-	County Dublin Vocational Education Committee
Emer Mulligan	-	Co-operation Fingal

Anita Morris	-	Fingal County Council
Bryan Murray	-	Fingal County Council
Keith Brock	-	Fingal Enterprise Board
Nuala Nic Giobuin	-	Dublin City Childcare Committee
Martin Clohessy	-	County Dublin Vocational Education Committee
Paul McEvoy	-	County Dublin Vocational Education Committee
Michael Moriarty	-	Irish Vocational Education Association
Jeanne Deegan	-	Rural Dublin LEADER

Appendix IV

Methodology

The paper draws on a large body of data collected between May 2005 and June 2006. The three main sources of data are:

(a)   organisational websites, annual reports (where available) and other publicly available material;
(b)   related policy and strategy documents (often prepared by consultants or other external sources);
(c)   interviews and discussions with local elected councillors, staff from local public agencies, academics, researchers and community activists.

A very substantial amount of information has been gathered but there have also been a number of unforeseen difficulties. For example, a number of local public agencies had not produced an annual report in some time. In the case of one agency, their most recent annual report related to 2001. In addition, a number of agencies were reluctant to release their most recent annual report. While they all eventually released the documentation, in one case it was incomplete and lacked the information relating to the agencies annual accounts. We find these occurrences, rare though they were, rather worrying given that:

(a)   the agencies were covered by the Freedom of Information Act, 1997;
(b)   we were in a position to "chase" the relevant information;
(c)   one of the reasons for the significant investment in

information and communications technologies in the public sector was the government's belief that it would facilitate a more engaged relationship between citizens and their public agencies.

However, in the majority of cases we found the agencies we contacted friendly and responsive and where they weren't able to provide the information we required they were usually able to point us in the right direction. In relation to the discussions and interviews we held with staff, community activists, academics and councillors, a number only spoke to us on condition of anonymity but all were generous with their time and comments and in general expressed a genuine desire to serve the public honourably and to the best of their ability (Appendix III).

Given the broad scope and variety of public and quasi-public agencies at work at the local level, it was helpful to devise an overview of the structure and pattern of the Irish local governance process. This is laid out in detail in Appendix I. The majority of the research was carried out by accessing relevant available literature on local government in Ireland, information held by the government's citizen information services and information from the websites of the organizations and agencies themselves. Further information for the overview was acquired through contacting relevant agencies and departments by telephone or by writing to them to request documentation. On completion of the overview analysis on the structure of local governance, further research was carried out on the pattern and nature of Irish local governance. This was achieved through a series of interviews and discussions, both via telephone and in person with senior political analysts, academics, politicians, civil servants and community activists. This qualitative research helped to expand on the questions raised by our initial overview work.

Support TASC
A Think Tank for Action on Social Change

> 'the limited development of think tanks is a striking feature [of Ireland]
> for such bodies could do much to focus new thinking about the country's
> future democratic and political development'

(REPORT TO THE
JOSEPH ROWNTREE CHARITABLE TRUST, 2002)

Ireland almost uniquely in Europe has relatively few think tanks of
any kind and, prior to the establishment of TASC, none whose sole
agenda is to foster new thinking on ways to create a more
progressive and equal society.

Your support is essential – to do its work TASC must keep a
distance from political and monetary pressure in order to protect
the independence of its agenda. If you would like to make a
contribution to TASC – A Think Tank for Action on Social
Change, please send your donation to the address below

DONATIONS TO:
TASC
A Think Tank for Action on Social Change
26 Sth Frederick St, Dublin 2.
Ph: 00353 1 6169050
Email:contact@tascnet.ie
www.tascnet.ie